KT-871-446

Extracts from Michael Caine's Moving Picture Show on pages 7, 22, 29, 35, 91, 101, 111, 121, 153 and 167.

Cover by Susan Mayer
Summer top from Marks & Spencer

▲52

81▶

▲172

◀91

Printed and published in Great Britain by D. C. Thomson & Co., Ltd., 185 Fleet Street, London EC4A 2HS © D. C. Thomson & Co., Ltd., 1990. While every reasonable care will be taken, neither D. C. Thomson & Co., Ltd., nor its agents will accept liability for loss or damage to colour transparencies or any other material submitted to this publication.

3

£3.05

SO really, it was the tadpole, I think, that did it.

The boys had brought them home in cardboard cups a week ago. No-one could think where and when the goldfish bowl was last seen, though everyone was quite sure they would remember it immediately. So the tadpoles stayed in the cardboard cups.

That afternoon I was planning to do some baking. I got out my mixing bowl and a big new recipe book and put them on the table. I suppose the recipe book must have toppled over, for the next moment everything was sopping and I was frantically scooping up wriggling black tadpoles.

I spooned them back into the cardboard cups, put away my baking

Go Out And KISS A STRANGER

Complete Story By ISOBEL STEWART

bowl and wet recipe book and searched for the goldfish bowl.

Half an hour later I found it and transferred the tadpoles. Then I had a bath, a cup of tea, and sat and thought . . .

I thought about tadpoles and goldfish bowls and my coming birthday. I thought about a folk-singer I'd known when I was 17. Everyone had thrown up their hands in horror and told me 24 was far too old for me.

I thought about my husband, John, who would soon be 42. And I thought about my children.

Sandra was 14 and inconsolable because her friend Margy needed a 34B bra and she was still wearing a 30A!

The twins, Roger and Tim, were 11 and fought all the time — with me, with their father, with Sandra, with each other, with everyone. Little Megan, by contrast, was a small, plump, serious six-year-old.

Then I thought about me. Nearly 35. I remembered wistfully that I hadn't been much older than Sandra when I fell in love with that folk-singer. Not much bigger, either.

Now, there always seemed to be a little more of me than I really wanted or expected. And I'd found two grey hairs last week.

I poured myself another cup of tea. What had happened to the years? Where had they gone? But more important, where had I gone — the Katherine Black I remembered so clearly? Who was this woman who had just mopped up 14 tadpoles from the kitchen floor?

I POURED myself a third cup of tea but there was no time to drink it.

I could hear the school bus coming along the road and then John's car turning in the drive. John teaches at the local school so the whole family comes home at the same time, but, except for Megan, the children won't hear of coming in their father's car.

It's only when they're all home that I realise how peaceful the day has been, even allowing for tadpoles on the kitchen floor . . . Or white mice loose in the boys' room, like the other day.

"Has Sasha had her kittens?" Sandra was asking me eagerly.

"You pushed me first, anyway," Roger said, scowling at his brother.

"I did not! You tripped me," Tim shot back.

"Marian Smith's mummy has a new little baby," Megan told me.

"I'll do some marking until you're ready," John said.

As usual, I took a deep breath.

"No," I told Sandra, "but Sasha's been looking in the linen cupboard." I glared at my sons. "I don't care who started it, but stop it, both of you." Then I bent down to Megan. "Is it a boy or a girl, darling?" And to John, "I'll be ready in half an hour. It's hardly worth you starting to mark. Couldn't you mend that gate instead?"

Then I remembered the tadpoles. "These tadpoles . . . " I said sternly.

"Where did you find the goldfish bowl?" Roger asked.

"Mum!" Tim was over looking at the tadpoles. "You've put them all together. Now we don't know which are mine and which are his."

"I had to put them together. I told you to get them out of those cardboard cups. They spilt so I had to put them all in the goldfish bowl."

Roger was counting the tadpoles. "She's lost one," he told Tim tersely.

They looked at me accusingly, their differences forgotten. Suddenly I was glad I hadn't done any baking. That missing tadpole . . .

"They'll never survive the change of water," Roger said.

"It must have been a terrible shock to them," Tim agreed.

I'd had enough then. "It was a terrible shock to me," I blurted out.

And then, to my surprise, I burst into tears. "I thought life held far more exciting possibilities for me than that, mopping up tadpoles from the kitchen floor," I wailed before I rushed into the bathroom and locked the door.

I heard the handle being tried. "Kath?" John asked cautiously. "Kath?"

"Go away," I told him. "Leave me alone."

"I can't," he said. "Megan wants to come in."

"She'll have to wait," I snapped.

"I can't," Megan said in a small voice.

"I gave in and opened the door. "Not even a separate toilet," I

☆☆☆☆☆☆☆☆☆☆☆☆☆☆☆☆☆☆☆☆☆☆☆☆☆☆

CHARLIE CHAPLIN

★★★★★★★★★★★★★

This extract and others on following pages taken from MICHAEL CAINE'S MOVING PICTURE SHOW published by Robson Books.

> ❝ It's said that when Charlie Chaplin's mother visited him on set and saw him in his Little Tramp costume for the first time she said, "Charlie, I must get you a new suit."
> The tramp costume — possibly the most famous of all screen costumes — was in fact assembled in a few minutes in the dressing-room at Mack Sennett's studio after Chaplin had been told to go and "get into a comedy make-up." The baggy trousers were borrowed from Fatty Arbuckle and the coat from Chester Conklin; both actors were hanging around the dressing-room at the time. The size 14 shoes and the bowler hat were loaned by others. Only the cane belonged to Chaplin himself. ❞

★★★★★★★★★★★★★★★★★★★★★★★★★★★★

said scathingly to John. "I told you we should have put in an extra toilet rather than spend money on that greenhouse."

Megan came out of the bathroom. "Are you better, Mummy?" she asked.

"I suppose so," I said.

"Better enough to make pink pudding for us?"

I made pink pudding. Sandra and the boys set the table and I found them looking at me as if they weren't sure what I was going to do next.

THAT night, after they had all gone to bed and everything was quiet except for Sandra's record player, John put aside the papers he was marking and turned to me. "Are you feeling better, love?" he asked.

I thought of the way the boys had washed the dishes for me, of Sandra asking me if I'd like to borrow her new lipstick, and of Megan asleep on her tummy, with her plump little bottom in the air.

"Yes," I told him honestly. "I feel much better now."

"Why don't you have a couple of days in town with Helen?" he suggested. "The change would do you good. Maybe you could get some new clothes for when we go on holiday."

I thought about it. My sister, Helen, and her husband, Andy, were always asking me to spend a few days with them. I could look round

Continued overleaf

A Fine Kettle Of Fish

And I soon found I had a fine sink, bath and basinful, says Marion Burkhill, when I decided to join the "School" of tropical fish enthusiasts!

A FEW years ago I decided to keep tropical fish. I set up my tank with all the appropriate paraphernalia, then when all was ready, I went to the best aquarist supplier I could find.

I wanted a small varied tank so decided to start off with Guppies, as they are supposed to be easy to keep and so ideal for beginners. I was then going to go on to Angel Fish, Neon Tetras and Swordtails, two of each, I thought, would be just fine.

In triumph I brought my two Guppies home, put them in the tank and stood back to admire them. They looked a bit lonely at first and were inclined to get lost among all the plants in that great big tank.

That was on the Friday! On the following Tuesday when I was feeding them I was more than surprised to see that there were six other tiny fishes only just visible. For a time I couldn't think where they had come from, then I thought they must have been in the net when the assistant had put the other two into my travelling jar. They were so small he probably hadn't noticed them.

Continued from previous page

the shops, have my hair done. Suddenly it seemed a good idea.

Though my family assured me they could manage, I felt bad about Megan. Her lips trembled as she said goodbye to me at the station, but Sandra took her hand and the boys stopped fighting long enough to cheer her up.

"Have a wonderful time, darling," John told me firmly, "and spend every penny."

At least, I thought as the train pulled out, that will be easier at Helen's since they have two bathrooms!

TWO bathrooms and both their children at boarding school. No tadpoles in the kitchen, no cat preparing for a confinement in the linen cupboard. Helen was four years younger than me, but I couldn't remember her ever being anything but organised, efficient and capable. She was still working, so I spent the daytime alone.

I enjoyed being on my own. I went to have my hair done but found the place very different from my hairdresser's at home — the stylist was a man.

"I found two grey hairs the other day," I told him, with that terrible desire to unburden myself that always comes over me at the

Two weeks later I was again feeding them when I noticed that there were two large fish, six medium-sized fish and ten tiny fish.

By this time I was really puzzled, then the light dawned.

I felt such a fool. I had asked for a *pair* of Guppie, not two as I had intended. I looked more closely at my fish and realised there was a difference. Some were very brightly coloured (these I learned later were the males), the silver-grey ones were females. One of my original two looked like a miniature barrage balloon and was simply bursting with young.

A MONTH later I had about fifty Guppies, and had to buy another large tank. I phoned all the pet shops and aquarists to see if anyone wanted some, but none of them wanted to know.

In despair, I phoned all my friends
Continued overleaf

hairdresser's. "And I had to mop up fourteen tadpoles from the kitchen floor. Actually, there were fifteen, I lost one."

"How very sad, madam," he murmured, not even blinking. "Now, what did you have in mind?"

I told him recklessly, "Just make me look different."

An hour later after I'd read an article on "How To Hold Your Husband" and another which asked threateningly if I was born before 1950, he took out the rollers and brushed my hair. I shut my eyes.

"There! Quite a difference!" he said enthusiastically.

It was undoubtedly a difference. My hair, which had had two hardly-visible grey hairs, now looked silver all over!

I was too stunned to say anything, even when I paid my bill. I went back to Helen's flat and waited for her to come home. Every so often I'd get up and catch a glimpse of myself in a mirror and gradually the surprise began to wear off. I decided cautiously that I liked it.

"Well, that's quite a change," Helen said when she came in. "I wonder what John will say."

I wondered, too, but I wasn't going to tell her that. "I like it," I said defiantly. "And tomorrow I'm going to buy some clothes. I can't ignore fashion any longer."

Continued overleaf

Continued from previous page
and relatives in the hope that I could give some of the fish away. It was all in vain! However, the baker did offer me some Harlequins and Swordtails in exchange, but by now I had gone off fish altogether.

I tried separating the sexes but by the time I recognised one from the other it was too late.

However, some aquarist enthusiasts came to my rescue. They were quite happy to take away their free Guppies, others were more serious, and had been trying for years to breed their fish. They would ask, in a rather aloof manner, "But what do you do?"

To which I could only reply, "I don't do anythng, they just do it themselves."

Eventually the fish spelled out their own doom. Because despite filters, aerating blocks, plants, oxygenating tablets and the like, the population explosion led to pollution that I just couldn't cope with.

Anyway by this time I'd enough and gave the remainder of my fish away. I've never had "tropicals" since, but have kept three veiltails and a goldfish for the past three years and they "behave" themselves very well! ■

Continued from previous page
And the next day, when I'd tried on the latest in a dimly-lit boutique, I decided I rather liked it, too.

Helen was having a party that night, so I thought I might as well stay and get used to my new clothes and my hair before I went home.

I COULDN'T think what had possessed Helen and Andy to invite all those guests. That night people were dancing in the dining-room, talking in the lounge, eating in the hall, drinking in the children's bedrooms. I felt I had been getting into a rut with my little dinners for six.

I was making my sixth round with snacks when the tray was suddenly taken from me.

"Time you started enjoying yourself, Cinderella," a deep voice said.

"Cinderella?" I asked, startled, looking up. And up.

He was very tall. Tall and bronzed, with fair hair.

"I don't feel like Cinderella," I told him. And I didn't. Every time I caught a glimpse of myself with my new hairstyle and my new dress I felt better and better.

"You don't look like Cinderella," he said, "but you're doing all the work." To my complete surprise, I blushed.

His name, he told me, was Pete. He was an engineer on leave from the Persian Gulf. He asked me my name and I told him.

"Katherine," he said, and I liked the way he said it. It was a long time since anyone had called me Katherine. I was Kath, Mum, Ma, Mummy, Auntie Kath or just "you."

"How did you come to know Helen and Andy?" Pete asked. "You seem different to their usual crowd."

"Helen is my sister," I said, feeling pleased.

"I didn't know Helen had a young sister," he said. "Have you come to make your fortune in the big city?"

I opened my mouth to say that Helen was actually *my* young sister, then I closed it again.

After a while, Pete asked me if I'd like to dance and I realised I wanted to.

We danced until I was laughing and breathless and then we sat on the stairs again and talked. He told me about his job in the Persian Gulf, then about his next job in South-West Africa. I was fascinated.

Suddenly he stopped talking and looked down at me, unsmiling, his blue eyes dark. Then he took my left hand in his and looked at the two rings.

"Is your husband here?" he asked. I shook my head.

"He must be either a fool or very trusting, letting you out on your own like this."

I felt myself colouring. "He thought I needed a change." I stood up abruptly. "I'd like to dance again, please."

We danced some more, and talked some more, and somehow I'd never felt so witty and amusing before.

More people joined us. I had them all laughing and clustering round me and I wondered dazedly if it was due to my hair, my new clothes, Pete beside me, or the brandy and ginger I was drinking.

But whatever it was, I could hardly believe it when Helen served hot coffee and I discovered it was two in the morning.

"Goodbye, Katherine," Pete said at the door. "Would your husband mind if I kissed you goodbye?"

He didn't wait for an answer. For a moment, his lips found mind and then he was gone.

"Your lipstick's smudged," Helen told me as I went into the kitchen. "Don't do these dishes now, Kath. Let's go to bed."

When I got into bed I was already half asleep, remembering how Pete had laughed at the things I'd said, how he had held me when we danced, how he had kissed me goodbye.

But in the morning, as I slowly woke up, the faint regret had gone. He had been nice, and I'd had fun, but somehow now Pete didn't seem quite real. I thought probably Cinderella had wondered if the Prince had been real the morning after the ball.

Continued on page 14

SETTING THE FUR FLYING . . .

Walking towards the shops the other day, I put up my umbrella to protect me from the drizzle. All of a sudden I felt a great weight thunder down on top of me.

I don't know who was more surprised — me or the terrified cat which had just made a flying leap off a nearby wall.

Now that saying "raining cats and dogs" has a new meaning for me. I just hope it's not a great Dane or a St Bernard that finishes the saying — and me — off!

cardigan
COOL

Materials Required. — Of **Sirdar Pom-Pom,** 8 (9, 9) x 50 gram balls main colour; 1 ball each of 2 contrast colours; one pair each of 4 mm and 5 mm (Nos. 8 and 6) knitting needles; 10 buttons.

For best results it is essential to use the recommended yarn. If you have difficulty in obtaining the yarn, write direct, enclosing a stamped addressed envelope, to the following address for stockists: Sirdar PLC, Flanshaw Lane, Alverthorpe, Wakefield, Yorkshire WF2 9ND.

Measurements. — To fit 86 (91, 97) cm, *34 (36, 38) inch,* bust; length, approximately 60 cm, *23½ inches;* sleeve seam, approximately, 41 cm, *16¼ inches.*

Tension. — 19 stitches and 27 rows to 10 cm, *4 inches,* measured over stocking-stitch using 5 mm needles.

Abbreviations. — K — knit; P — purl; st.(s) — stitch(es); y.r.n. — yarn round needle; tog. — together; st.-st. — stocking-stitch; cm — centimetres; ins — inches; M — main colour; A — 1st Contrast; B — 2nd Contrast.

N.B. Figures in brackets ( ) refer

to the larger sizes; where only one figure is given, this refers to all sizes. Figures in square brackets [ ] are worked the number of times stated. When working in more than one colour, use separate small balls of yarn for each area of colour and twist yarns where they join on every row to avoid holes.

Back.

Using 4 mm needles and M, cast on 81 (85, 89) sts.

1st row (right side). — [K1, P1] to last st., K1.

2nd row. — [P1, K1] to last st., P1.

Repeat these 2 rows for 6 cm, 2¼ ins, ending with a 2nd row and increase 19 (21, 23) sts. evenly across last row — 100 (106, 112) sts.

Change to 5 mm needles.

Work in st.-st., starting with a knit row and work in colour sequence as follows:

1st and 2nd rows. — 11 (14, 17)M, 1A, 19M, 1B, 36M, 1B, 19M, 1A, 11 (14, 17)M.

3rd and 4th rows. — 10 (13, 16)M, 3A, 17M, 2B, 36M, 2B, 17M, 3A, 10 (13, 16)M.

5th and 6th rows. — 9 (12, 15)M, 5A, 15M, 3B, 36M, 3B, 15M, 5A, 9 (12, 15)M.

7th and 8th rows. — 8 (11, 14)M, 7A, 13M, 4B, 36M, 4B, 13M, 7A, 8 (11, 14)M.

9th and 10th rows. — 7 (10, 13)M, 9A, 11M, 5B, 36M, 5B, 11M, 9A, 7 (10, 13)M.

11th and 12th rows. — 6 (9, 12)M, 11A, 9M, 6B, 36M, 6B, 9M, 11A, 6 (9, 12)M.

13th and 14th rows. — 5 (8, 11)M, 13A, 7M, 7B, 36M, 7B, 7M, 13A, 5 (8, 11)M.

15th and 16th rows. — As 11th and 12th rows.

17th and 18th rows. — As 9th and 10th rows.

19th and 20th rows. — As 7th and 8th rows.

21st and 22nd rows. — As 5th and 6th rows.

23rd and 24th rows. — As 3rd and 4th rows.

These 24 rows form the pattern, repeat them 5 times more then 1st and 2nd rows once.

Next row. — Using M, cast off 33 (36, 39) sts., K34 sts. (including st. on needle), cast off 33 (36, 39) sts. Leave the 34 sts. on a holder.

Right Front.

Using 4 mm needles and M, cast on 39 (43, 45) sts. and work 6 cm, 2¼ ins, in rib as for back, increasing 9 (8, 9) sts. evenly across last row — 48 (51, 54) sts.

Change to 5 mm needles.

Continue in st.-st., starting with a knit row and work in colour sequence as follows.

1st row. — 16M, 1B, 19M, 1A, 11 (14, 17)M.

2nd row. — 11 (14, 17)M, 1A, 19M, 1B, 16M.

3rd row. — 16M, 2B, 17M, 3A, 10 (13, 16)M.

4th row. — 10 (13, 16)M, 3A, 17M, 2B, 16M.

Continue as for back until work is 20 rows shorter than back.

Shape Neck.

Cast off 6 sts. at beginning of next row then decrease one st. at neck edge on every row until 33 (36, 39) sts. remain.

Continue until work measures same as back. Cast off.

Continued overleaf

13

Continued from previous page

Left Front.

Work as right front, reversing shaping, noting that 1st row will read: 11 (14, 17)M, 1A, 19M, 1B, 16M.

Sleeves (Both Alike).

Using 4 mm needles and M, cast on 39 (41, 43) sts. and work 5 cm, *2 ins*, in rib as for back, increasing 14 sts. evenly across last row — 53 (55, 57) sts.

Change to 5 mm needles.

Continue in st.-st., starting with a knit row and work in colour sequence as follows:

1st and 2nd rows. — 26 (27, 28)M, 1B, 26 (27, 28)M.

3rd and 4th rows. — 25 (26, 27)M, 3B, 25 (26, 27)M.

Continue as for back but working only diamond pattern in B *at the same time* increase one st. at each end of the 5th and every following 4th row, taking extra sts. into M, until there are 99 (101, 103) sts.

Work 5 more rows thus ending with a 2nd pattern row.

Cast off.

Neckband.

Join shoulder seams. Using 4 mm needles and M, with right side facing, pick up and K23 sts. up right front neck, K34 sts. from back holder (decreasing one st. in centre), then pick up and K23 sts. down left front neck — 79 sts.

Starting with a 2nd row, work 5 rows in rib as for back.

Cast off in rib.

Left Front Band: Using 4 mm needles and M, cast on 7 sts.

1st row. — K2, [P1, K1] twice, K1.

2nd row. — [K1, P1] 3 times, K1.

Repeat these 2 rows until band, when slightly stretched, fits up right front. Cast off in rib.

Mark position of 10 buttons, first 2 cm, *¾ inch*, from lower edge, 10th 2 cm, *¾ inch*, from upper edge with 8 more spaced evenly between.

Right Front Band: Work as for left front band, making buttonholes to correspond with markings, on right-side rows as follows: K2, P1, y.r.n., P2 tog., K2.

To Make Up.

Sew in sleeves, placing centre of sleeves to shoulder seams. Join side and sleeve seams. Sew on front bands. Sew on buttons. Do not press.

Continued from page 11

All at once I couldn't wait to get home. I jumped out of bed and dressed quickly.

The train journey seemed to take ages. I wondered how John would like my hair and if Sandra would approve of my dress.

THEY were all waiting at the station, John holding Megan up on his shoulder, the boys with the dog on his lead, Sandra forgetting she was 14 and sophisticated and jumping up and down with excitement.

"I like your hair, love," John said.

"All the kittens are white this time," said Sandra.

"I'm glad you're home," Megan whispered.

"We got more tadpoles," Roger informed me.

"And we're going to swop them for guinea-pigs as soon as they're frogs," Tim added.

"Let's go home," John said, laughing. "Your mother's bewildered. Let her get used to you all again gradually."

The house was shining and spotless. Sandra made tea, the boys carried in my luggage, and Megan sat on my knee. I kept feeling John's eyes on me and something in the way he was looking at me made me feel uncomfortable — nicely uncomfortable, if you know what I mean.

When we were going to the linen cupboard to see the kittens, John put his arm around me.

"I'm glad you're home," he said quietly. "It isn't the same without you." And then he kissed me, a long, quiet, loving kiss.
"I've always wanted to kiss a blonde," he murmured.

"They're kissing," I heard Roger say disgustedly. "Megan, tell them to come and see the kittens."

Laughing, we drew apart and went to the maternity ward. Sasha lay on the bottom shelf, her paws round four snow-white kittens.

I touched them gently. "They're beautiful," I told her, "and you're a very clever cat to have such lovely babies."

"Can we keep one, Mummy?" Sandra asked. "Just one?"

"Then Sasha won't be so sad when the other kittens go," Megan pointed out.

"All right, just one," I agreed rashly, knowing that when the time came they'd tell me that one kitten would be very lonely, couldn't we just keep two?

The dog was scratching on the door, so we went out and convinced him that we loved him just as much as we loved the kittens. Then the boys took me to see their tadpoles.

"Look," Roger said proudly.

I looked. There seemed to be a hundred tadpoles in the goldfish bowl.

"Where are you going to keep them when they become frogs?" I asked faintly.

DOUBLE MEANING

I hadn't much luck with my panti-hose, having gone through several pairs in a very short time.

When I went to buy a new pair, the shop assistant was sympathetic, but I thought her words were not very well chosen when she put the tights in a bag and said, "I do hope you get a good run in these!"

The boys looked surprised. "In the kitchen, of course, Mum," Tim told me. He pointed out that I'd have to be ready to catch each frog as it jumped out and they'd a box ready in case this happened while they were at school.

"You needn't worry," Roger assured me. "By that time they'll be so tame they'll jump right into your hand."

"That's just what I'm afraid of," I told them.

Above their heads, my eyes met John's and we began to laugh. And I thought, looking around, that all the thrilling possibilities life could ever hold were right here in my own kitchen.

——————— ✳ **THE END** ✳ ———————

In many ways her life was like the necklace — each part precious in itself but with one important link missing.

Complete Story by PAMELA SPECK

OLD Mr Northcott cleared his throat. He removed the spectacles that were balanced on the tip of his nose and folded them carefully, to signify that his reading of the will had come to an end. Clarissa Baines rose, but he restrained her with a wave of his hand.

"Sit down, Clarissa, my dear. There's just one thing more."

She sat quietly, her hands held still in her lap as she had been taught so many years ago at school.

Mr Northcott went on, tempering the dry, official voice he had used before and sounding more like what he was — an old friend of Clarissa's family.

The Magic Necklace

"Your mother wrote to me a few weeks before she died," he said. "I have the letter here . . . there was something she wanted done.

"Not a very important thing, but she didn't want to bother you at that time . . ."

Clarissa understood. That was just like Mother.

"It seems an odd request. But then I am sure you will understand more about it than I do. Your mother spoke of a string of beads she had treasured for years — er — *magic* beads are the words she used. Do you know what she means?"

Clarissa smiled; she would have laughed if it hadn't been such a solemn occasion. She knew the ones he meant. They were the beads her father had bought her mother years ago when they had met and fallen in love in Venice.

He had bought her other, more expensive pieces of jewellery in the years that followed, but she had cherished the beads more than anything else.

"From the minute I had them," she used to say, "nice things happened to me."

They were the ones she had worn on anniversaries and birthdays, the ones she had put away in a velvet case when Clarissa's father

B

died, taking them out only to look at and remember. It was almost as though she felt nothing quite so nice could happen to her again.

"I do indeed, Mr Northcott," Clarissa said at last. "I was never allowed to wear them. Mother let me wear all her jewellery but never the beads. It wasn't that they were valuable, I suppose they are almost worthless really.

"Their value is purely sentimental. And as for their being magic . . . !" She smiled at him. "Well, you knew Mother . . . it was just a little family joke."

"They don't appear to have been a joke to your mother, Clarissa. They evidently meant a great deal to her. She mentioned in her letter that the string had been broken . . . ."

"Broken . . . ?" Clarissa was startled. Her mother had never mentioned that! Surely she would have done so . . . those beads were more precious to her than the Crown Jewels!

"Broken," Mr Northcott continued, looking at her reproachfully. She was not expected to interrupt. "And what's more, some of the beads were lost."

Clarissa restrained a gasp, looking at him in amazement. Why had her mother never mentioned it to her? She had had plenty opportunity in the times they had shared during her illness.

"She was anxious that the beads should be replaced and re-strung as soon as possible, and that you should start wearing them right away . . ." Again, the self-conscious "hmmm."

"Your mother seemed convinced that the beads were endowed with special qualities which bestowed happiness and good fortune on their wearer.

"She was very anxious that you should be so blessed . . . her actual words were 'I want nice things to happen to Clarissa now!'

"As I say, my dear, it is only a small thing that your mother has asked, but I know you will undertake to do it." He fell silent and smiled at her, waiting for her answer.

"Of course I'll do as Mother wanted, Mr Northcott, although it does seem strange."

"I know, my dear," he said slowly. "I know." Then he folded his spectacles again, and Clarissa rose and said goodbye.

IT was difficult for Clarissa to fully accept that her mother no longer needed her. No-one needed her. She was alone.

For 15 years she had stayed at home to nurse her mother. Now, the friends she'd once had were married and scattered, nothing remaining but faded photographs and occasional letters. And this had also worried her mother.

"You should get out, Clarissa," she used to say. "Circulate a bit, meet people, make friends. Join a drama group — *do* something.

"Never mind me — the vicar's wife keeps offering to stay, everyone does. Why, you don't know a soul now!"

"Mother, that isn't true!" she'd reply. "I get out a lot — I go to the library and do the shopping, and I know lots of people!"

The older woman would then try a different approach.

"Has it occurred to you that I might not enjoy watching the

television with you evening after evening? That I might want to be alone?"

But Clarissa knew that her mother was only putting it on, so she just smiled and went about what she was doing. There was simply no point getting involved in useless arguments . . .

Perhaps her mother had been right, Clarissa thought now, sitting in the darkened living-room. She'd been so content looking after her, she hadn't realised how retiring she'd become herself.

Perhaps she should get herself some sort of job where she would meet people as her mother had wanted — after she had seen about her mother's beads.

Mother's magic beads . . . she smiled to herself in the darkness. It had always amused her to think that her mother really believed those beads possessed some sort of magical powers. She'd heard the story so many times . . .

★   ★   ★   ★

It happened one summer, many years ago, when her mother was a girl. She'd been holidaying in Venice and had caught sight of something sparkling in a jeweller's shop.

"They were glinting in the sun, almost beckoning to me," she'd say, remembering that summer. "I went over to have a closer look. A young man was standing by the window. He seemed to be looking at them too. 'They're very beautiful, aren't they?' he said, turning to me. Then he said, 'You know, they're the exact colour of your eyes . . .'

"I didn't know what to say then, but we met frequently after that — exploring the old city, admiring its treasures, being rowed by singing gondoliers . . . it was like a dream.

"On the last night of our holiday, he gave me the beads that had brought us together. And then, of course, I married him."

CLARISSA had always understood why her mother had loved them, and she knew she would have to get them fixed. She decided to take them to the best jeweller's in town, although she realised they were only glass and not the sort of thing jewellers handled. But perhaps someone could advise her of the best place to take them.

The journey to town didn't bother her this time. She felt an old hand at it, having done it only the day before. She'd also gone through her wardrobe and picked out something smart to wear — it wouldn't do to go into the shop looking like a cranky old maid.

The shop she had chosen had thick carpets and concealed lighting. There was no-one else there. She asked for the manager and waited nervously while he came, aware of the glitter of expensive jewellery around her.

What would he think of Mother's glass beads . . . ? Perhaps she had chosen the wrong shop. Perhaps he would be amused and patronising . . . Panic rose inside her.

But when he came, he took her into his office and listened politely to her story. Then he took the beads from her with hands as gentle as her own.

Lying down on the polished surface of his desk, with the special lamp he had switched on shining down on them, they looked every bit as beautiful and precious as the diamonds that glittered in the glass cases. Perfectly graded in size and colour, each bead shone with every imaginable shade of blue.

"Venetian glass beads," he murmured. "You don't see many of them nowadays. What incredibly beautiful shades!"

Clarissa was alarmed.

"You don't think they'll be difficult to match, do you?" she asked anxiously.

"I wouldn't like to hazard a guess," he replied, still looking at them. "They're out of my province really . . . but I do know someone who might be able to help you.

"He's an antique dealer and has quite a collection of costume jewellery. If anyone can help you, he can. I've got his card here."

She was delighted. "Thank you so much," she said. "You've been so kind . . ." Her voice faltered as she saw the address. It was in Manchester.

"Is something the matter?" he asked, looking up at her then.

"N — no, nothing at all," she replied.

CROSSED LINES

My son is in the Royal Navy, and on a recent visit to Scandinavia met a very pretty Norwegian girl, but when he turned up late for his second date with her she got angry.

He let her complain for a bit in her broken English, and when he thought she had gone on long enough he said:

"Are you finished?"

"No," came her reply. "I've told you — I'm Norwegian."

This remark set him falling about laughing, and to this day the poor girl still doesn't know why!

She couldn't let him see how taken aback she was at the thought of going all that way. She was sure that the sort of woman he was used to wouldn't go to pieces at the idea of a train journey. She wished suddenly that she wasn't quite so faded and mouselike.

She looked up, and discovered that he was looking at her intently.

"These beads," he said. "Do you realise that they match the colour of your eyes exactly!"

She remembered that someone had said almost the same words to a girl outside a jeweller's shop many years before.

"My father bought them for that same reason — because they matched my mother's eyes," she told him.

"I see . . ." he said. They both fell silent . . .

"Look, you must let me know how you get on in Manchester," he said hurriedly. "Whether my friend is any help. If not, I'll give it some more thought. If you let me have your address I'll let you know if I think of anything. I fully realise how much these beads must mean to you now."

Clarissa was touched. He was so concerned. It would be selfish of her not to go to Manchester when people were being so helpful.

And she really should buy some new clothes before going. She hadn't realised how hopelessly dowdy she looked. Her mother had always enjoyed poring over magazines, and urged her to get fashionable things, but there hadn't been any point as she never went anywhere.

And her hair — perhaps she ought to have that done. That was something else her mother had gone on about . . .

AND so it was, that by the time she arrived to see Mr Myers, the antique dealer in Manchester, she wasn't quite the same Clarissa whom his friend, Don Roberts, had phoned about in advance.

"Hopelessly spinsterish but rather nice," was how he described her. But this Clarissa was as fashionable as anybody Mr Myers had met.

Unfortunately he couldn't help Clarissa either.

"They stopped making these beads at the beginning of the war," he told her. "We come across them very seldom now. They're going to be very difficult to replace indeed."

Clarissa found it hard to believe. "But — they're just cheap trinkets, really!" she exclaimed.

"It's because they were once so cheap that they are so rare now," he told her. "Things like these were thrown away when they were broken because they were so easy to replace.

"It's a pity you couldn't manage a trip to Venice. You'd stand a better chance of turning up something there than in this country."

"*Venice*," she repeated weakly.

"Yes. I've got some contacts there . . ."

She rose hastily. "Th-thank you," she said, "I'll have to think about it. I don't think it's worth going to all that bother. I . . ."

He looked surprised. "I got the impression from Don that this was very important to you. That you were prepared to go to any length."

She sat down again. "Yes," she said slowly. "It *is* important."

It didn't matter if Mr Myers knew how timid she really was. She didn't want to impress him as, oddly enough, she had wanted to impress Don Roberts. She decided to be quite honest.

"You see . . . I haven't been anywhere outside our village for the past fifteen years. I have qualms about meeting strange people and going to strange places. I just can't help it.

"Even though I'm determined to do everything I can to replace Mother's beads, it does take me a little while to make up my mind. I haven't made any really big decisions for years . . . and going abroad would be a very big decision for me. You do understand, don't you?"

She looked pleadingly at him. She must sound ridiculous, a woman of her age!

But he only smiled broadly.

MARILYN MONROE

★ ★

‘ Making *Some Like It Hot* was torture for Tony Curtis and Jack Lemmon. Dressed in frocks and high heels, they had to wait hours for Marilyn Monroe to arrive on set and film scenes with them. And when she did come she sometimes had trouble remembering the words. For one scene in which her only line was, "Where's the bourbon?" she needed 40 takes. And for another, in which Tony Curtis had to chew the meat from a chicken bone, she took 42. Apparently Curtis couldn't look at a chicken for months afterwards. ’

★ ★

Continued from previous page

"Of course I understand," he said. "And that's all the more reason why you should go to Italy. You won't just be looking for a few beads, you'll be having a holiday with a purpose — and doing yourself the world of good. Don't you agree?"

Clarissa could only nod. Her life seemed to have taken an unexpected turn since her mother died. Did she ever imagine when she lost those beads — and when she wrote asking for them to be replaced — that this would happen? Clarissa thought not.

Her mother had never liked being any trouble.

EXCITEMENT rose in her as she planned for her holiday on the way home in the train. Her relatives had encouraged her to take a holiday when her mother died; they would be surprised to hear the sort of holiday she was going to have. Her mother had always spoken of Italy with nostalgia . . . now she was going to see for herself.

The house didn't seem quite so empty when she got back, especially when the phone started to ring. It was Don Roberts from the jeweller's shop and he seemed surprised and pleased that she remembered him.

Did she know there was an exhibition of theatrical and costume jewellery in her area? It was something she really ought to see. There would be people there who might be able to help her. He knew a few of them himself and would be happy to introduce her.

Clarissa put the phone down excitedly and went to look through her dresses. He'd mentioned something about a drink after the exhibition. She had to look well. The dark blue dress perhaps, with that long string of flapper pearls her mother had loved so much.

She reached into her mother's old jewel case for them and found to her surprise that the bottom of the case was loose. Just the inner, velvet-covered bit — the outside was quite intact. It was almost as though someone had prised it loose.

She lifted it gently, looking in wonder at the small envelope under it and in even greater wonder at what it contained.

Six perfectly-graded glass beads in every imaginable shade of blue . . .

She laughed aloud in her relief at finding them. Mother's little bits of magic — they weren't lost after all! They'd been here all this time.

And all the while she'd been chasing over town, going up north, even arranging to spend a few weeks in Italy! Her mother must have put them away so carefully she'd forgotten where they were.

Or had she?

It didn't sound like her at all. She'd had a razor-sharp mind in spite of her illness, and could think things out so much better than other people. There must be some other explanation.

Could this be yet another of her weird and wonderful get-Clarissa-out-and-about schemes?

She called Mr Northcott right away. "You'll never guess!" she told him. "I've been chasing halfway round the country and almost started to look in another, and now I've found Mother's beads right here!"

She paused. "You haven't been quite fair with me, have you, Mr Northcott? I've got a feeling you knew where they were all the time!"

He didn't answer her question, and indeed didn't sound the least bit surprised. "Have you, Clarissa?" he asked mildly. "And tell me, what else have you found — besides the beads?"

"What else . . . ?" She stopped.

What else had she found?

SHE had found so many people willing and happy to help her, she had found the courage to arrange a holiday in a sunny land, and she had found a friend to take her out this evening when no doubt she would make more friends.

A life outside these four walls, exactly as her mother would have wished . . .

"I'll call in at the office tomorrow and tell you about it," she promised. "I can't stop now, I'm just going out for the evening."

She could hear the smile in his voice as he said goodbye.

She rose hurriedly to go and change. She couldn't imagine why her mother had been so concerned about leaving her alone, so worried that she wouldn't go out and make friends. It was the easiest thing in the world . . .

The beads sparkled on her dressing-table, caught by a shaft of afternoon sunlight. so many nice things were happening to her and she hadn't even started wearing them . . . could her mother have been right after all?

Could they have just the *slightest* touch of magic . . . ?

——————— * **THE END** * ———————

As a boy, in wartime, I'd been evacuated up north into a family of strangers. It was here I met "Aunt" Kath, and I learned the meaning of love . . .

ALWAYS IN MY HEART

Complete Story By
MERVYN WATKINS

CAREFULLY I spread out the wrapping paper on the living-room table and cut a piece the size I needed. Then I took the toby jug from its box to have one last look at it before I wrapped it up.

My 14-year-old daughter, Kathleen, had been watching me with interest and some amusement. Now she came over and sat beside me.

"Is that another one?" she asked, a smile playing on her face.

"Yes," I said.

"Can I see it?"

I held the toby jug out to her and carefully she took it from me.

"I can't understand it," she said, "Every year on her birthday, you

send her a toby jug — why, Dad?"

"Well, that's a long story," I began. "And it happened a long time ago . . ."

"Tell her, John," a voice behind me said.

I turned to see my wife, Mary, standing at the door.

"All right," I said, and so hesitatingly at first, stumbling for the right words, my mind slipped back down the years . . .

★　　　★　　　★　　　★

When I was a lad, living in wartime London I was evacuated up north to a small mining village beside the sea. There, I stayed with the Rudkin family. But although I was made welcome there were no other London evacuees within miles and I always felt like an intruder. Except with Aunt Kath.

The Rudkins were kind, hard-working folk and honest as the day was long. But Jack Rudkin's word was law and even his three sons, hefty colliers though they were, went in fear of their father.

He would read no book but the Bible and blamed the Second World War on man's reluctance to work hard. It wasn't a philosophy that I appreciated. All I knew was that war had forced my father to go away and fight overseas. My father was a widower so I'd had to go and live with my aunt. But she was killed in the Blitz . . .

I WAS alone and lost the day I arrived at the strange northern station with only my suitcase, and an identity tag marked *John Hemming* round my neck. Immediately I looked upon Kath Rudkin as my guardian angel.

I say "angel" because Kath was fair skinned and gentle with blonde hair which gleamed gold even on the most dismal day.

And there were plenty of dismal days for me as an evacuee. There were times when life didn't seem worth living and times when I planned to stow away on a boat and cross the Channel to find my father.

Aunt Kath was the only person to understand my feelings. It seemed to me, she was a kind of intruder, too, even in her own home.

The Rudkins lived in two white-washed pit cottages converted into one dwelling. Mrs Rudkin's cooking was good and she was always kind to me, but I always felt rather uncomfortable unless her daughter, Kath, was there. Kath seemed to be almost as unhappy as myself.

I never understood why she didn't get on with her father. He was almost short with her and seemed to resent her presence. Young as I was, I knew that Kath didn't feel at home in her father's house. She didn't seem to belong, and nothing belonged to her. Except the two toby jugs.

The toby jugs fascinated me. They stood on Kath's dressing-table and I first saw them when Mrs Rudkin asked me to wake Kath one morning after the men had gone to the pit. Kath had been sleeping on in the mornings when I first arrived and I thought it was to avoid her father.

That morning I overheard him say, "Is that lass still abed?"

And Mrs Rudkin answered, "Leave her just now, Jack. She has to get her strength back."

"She'll have to get up in the morning when she starts work again!" Jack Rudkin growled back.

Then Mrs Rudkin saw me standing in the doorway. "John," she said. "Can you tell Kath her breakfast's ready, if she wants it."

I felt troubled. I'd grown to depend on Kath's company in the daytime. Things would be different if she was working. I knocked on her door and she called out, "Come in."

She wasn't in bed. She was sitting at the window fully dressed, staring across the village towards the sea. When she turned round, I could see the faraway yearning look in her eyes.

"Oh, it's you, John," she said.

"What are you looking at, Aunt Kath?" I asked, feeling shy about being in her room.

"Oh, the shore and the sea, John, and whatever there is beyond . . ." Her voice tailed off and she looked away again.

"Can I see?"

"Yes, John. Come and have a look."

I stood at the window listening to my own heart. The sea was wild and the same pewter grey colour as the sky.

"What can you see?" she asked.

"Well, there's colliers walking along the shore to the pit . . . and the sea's all rough . . ."

"But what can you see beyond that?"

"I . . . I can see my father fighting," I answered slowly. "He's not really fighting though. He can't — in a P.O.W. camp."

"Be thankful at least that you get letters from him sometimes, John. It's hard for you I know. But the war will be over one day . . . then your dad will come back safe to you."

I NODDED, keeping my eyes on the sea because there were tears in her eyes and I didn't know what to do when a woman was crying. I'd never seen a woman cry before.

MUSICAL S O S

My friend's budgie had been missing all day and the family had searched everywhere, without success.

Sadly, they went to bed, my friend carrying her portable radio.

After she had switched on, she thought she heard a faint chirruping from somewhere in the house.

The search was on again and at last Joey was found — inside a vase on the mantelpiece in the front room!

Joey had always loved to hear music and the music from the radio had helped to revive his spirits just in time. They gently eased him out of the vase and he was none the worse for his experience.

"Mrs Rudkin says your breakfast's ready if you want it," I said to change the subject.

"Thanks, John. But I'm not hungry."

I was about to leave the room when I noticed the toby jugs. I couldn't take my eyes off them.

"You like them?" Aunt Kath asked.

"They're terrific." And I knew from her expression that she thought so too. "Have a look at them," she invited, "but please be careful. They're fragile — and very precious."

Nervously I picked up one of the blue-coated toby jugs. "They're like real men," I enthused, studying the red-faced toby with the beaming smile, twinkling eyes and a tricorn hat.

"They are real to me, John. And they remind me of peaceful, happy times," she said softly.

"Who . . . who gave them to you?" I asked.

Her face clouded over. "A friend," she replied.

She took the toby jug from me and replaced it on the dressing-table. Then more to herself than to me she whispered, "It was to be the start of a collection. A special collection to go on and on over the years . . ."

She broke off with a little frown as though she'd forgotten I was in the room.

"Well, John. How about a brisk walk along the shore?" she said. Suddenly bright, she reached for her coat . . .

WE walked along the shore sometimes struggling to keep our balance against the strong wind. The colliery looked grim and stark.

"Are you going back to work soon, Aunt Kath?" I asked. She stopped suddenly. I was afraid I'd said something to offend her.

"I heard Mr Rudkin saying something . . ." I faltered.

Anger flashed in her eyes.

"Oh, I see!" she said.

I felt the colour burning my cheeks, but her anger wasn't against me.

"It's all right, John." She ruffled my hair. "I was just thinking something else. Are you happy here with us?"

"I'm happy with you," I admitted, my face getting even redder.

Gently she lifted my chin with her fingers. They were warm and soft and I thought she was the most beautiful woman in the world.

"Yes, John," she said. I'll be going back to work again soon. But I'll be back at six o'clock each day," she explained. "Then you and I can go for walks together."

Unconsoled, I asked, "Where will you be working?"

"At the munitions factory. It's ten miles from here and I have to go by bus.

"Do you *have* to go to work?" I implored her.

"I have to help with the war effort, John."

"What's munitions, anyway."

"It's like ammunition," she explained quietly. "For fighting the enemy."

I pictured my father — captured by the Germans. Munitions didn't make any sense to me right then.

"Why aren't you working now then?"

It was a long time before she answered. "I haven't been well. I — I'd only just come out of hospital when you arrived."

I didn't like to ask why she'd been in hospital.

"Are you better now?"

She smiled, a sad sort of smile. "You've made me feel a lot better. I'll be starting work at the factory on Monday."

"Why can't you stay at home, like Mrs Rudkin?" I ventured.

She laughed. "My mam has a full-time job looking after a big family, John. Besides, I'm better off out of the house."

I didn't question that, because suddenly Kath looked angry again. We walked on as far as the colliery, but turned back when it started to rain.

"How old are you, Aunt Kath?" I asked.

She glanced at me quickly and smiled. "A man shouldn't ask a lady such questions, John Hemming," she protested. "But let's say that I won't see thirty again."

I'd been pondering one question ever since I'd first seen her. "Why aren't you married then if you're over thirty?" I asked.

She looked away. "Not all women get married, John," she answered.

"But you're so — well, pretty. If I was a man I'd marry you."

She stopped and smiled again. "Thank you, John Hemming. That's one of the nicest things anyone ever said to me. But don't be in a hurry to grow up. Growing up lasts for ever. Enjoy being a child, then one day you'll be a fine man."

I didn't understand her, but as we walked back to the house Kath made me promise that when she started work I'd make the most of my days playing with the other children in the village. I promised, but only because she'd asked me to . . .

THE days without Aunt Kath were empty and endless. I tried playing with the local children and on the whole they were a friendly lot. Except for a boy called Billy Marvin.

He had dark greasy hair and his clothes were always torn or patched. He seemed dedicated to making my life a misery. He called me a Cockney and a cissy and lots of other horrible things, too.

Continued on page 34

☆☆☆☆☆☆☆☆☆☆☆☆☆☆☆☆☆☆☆☆☆☆☆☆☆☆☆☆

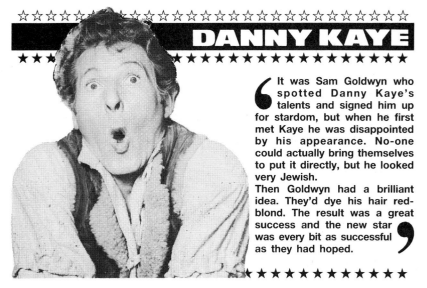

DANNY KAYE

★★★ ★★★★★★★★★★★★★★★★★

‘ It was Sam Goldwyn who spotted Danny Kaye's talents and signed him up for stardom, but when he first met Kaye he was disappointed by his appearance. No-one could actually bring themselves to put it directly, but he looked very Jewish.

Then Goldwyn had a brilliant idea. They'd dye his hair red-blond. The result was a great success and the new star was every bit as successful as they had hoped. ’

★★★★★★★★★★★★★★

The Taming Of EBENEZER

Quite a handful — that was my first impression of Ebenezer, says Rosemary Alexander. In fact, it took me almost a week before that wild snarling cat would let me near enough to touch him!

EBENEZER crept into our lives one Saturday morning, his tabby coat tattered and torn. He trusted no-one — and with very good reason.

Thrown from a car when little more than a kitten, he had lived wild on the Common, until an RSPCA inspector captured him.

We happened to be visiting the home after he had just been brought in. When his amber eyes met mine I recognised a kindred spirit, and decided to adopt him. He was too distraught to acknowledge the bond, and merely demonstrated his lack of gratitude for our interest by scratching my daughter's neck as she tried to lift him into a pet carrier!

On the journey home Ebenezer was ominously quiet. When we opened the lid and saw his eyes widen with terror, we played safe and checked our natural instinct to caress him. Once home, we checked all the doors and windows, then left him alone in the kitchen to settle down.

Within easy reach I'd put a comfortable bed, a saucer of pilchards, a dish of water, and a cinder tray . . . so Ebby could see he was welcome.

An hour or so later, we looked in on him to find that the pet carrier was empty, the pilchards untouched, and the bed unoccupied — Ebby had vanished!

We searched every nook and cranny for him, opened cupboards, peered in the coal scuttle, pulled out drawers, but Ebby had definitely fled. It was as though he had never existed.

For a moment, we succumbed to the nightmare sensation that he had been nothing more than a figment of our imagination!

Commonsense reminded me that cats don't just vanish into the blue, so after accusing each other of carelessness, despite evidence to the contrary, there was little we could do except retire to bed. Our well-meant plan to adopt a wild "orphan" had been a fiasco.

Next morning, I was first downstairs. The kitchen still had a silent, deserted air but, to my amazement,

Continued overleaf

Continued from previous page

the pilchards had gone, and the cinder tray had been put to its rightful purpose.

I rushed upstairs to tell the family and, for once, I had no difficulty in getting the usual sleepyheads to rise.

We continued our search for Ebenezer, and searched every cupboard, drawer and receptacle likely to attract a fugitive cat.

Then my daughter had a brainwave. We had forgotten to look behind the cooker! The space there is quite large, but thick with dust and grease because we can only clean it out if the cooker is dismantled.

With difficulty we peered round the cooker and could just make out two amber eyes peering up from the murky depths. Ebby had been found! But that was the extent of our triumph.

EVERYTHING we tried failed to move him and he remained there all day. Now and then, my daughter managed to tempt him into the gap alongside the boiler with milk in a teaspoon, held at arm's length.

Occasionally, his nose or the tip of a whisker appeared round the back of the cooker. That was all.

Our Sunday joint presented the next big problem. We were all looking forward to a nice roast, yet if we put the oven on we'd be in danger of roasting Ebby, too.

By tea-time our appetites forced us to mount a full-scale operation to dislodge the lone squatter. Inch by inch, using milk as bait, we lured him forwards, but just when we were on the point of catching him a sneeze, a knock at the door, our dog barking, or the ring of the telephone sent him cringing back.

But at last he emerged and we quickly slipped a short plank over the entrance to his retreat.

Ebby was furious and tore across the kitchen, then crouched in the darkest corner of the alcove, by the back door, spitting defiance. "Operation Dislodgement" had done absolutely nothing to improve his opinion of the human race.

When we moved his dishes and bed closer to him Ebby snarled at us in loathing. However, at least we could see him now, which was an improvement. Nevertheless for the next two days he lost no chance to remind us of his dislike.

He stayed by the back door, spitting at us whenever we appeared. We even had to redirect tradesmen to the front door.

As though aware we had lovingly made it up for him, he spurned his comfortable bed. But he ate heartily and, in matters of personal hygiene, his behaviour was beyond reproach.

On Tuesday evening we were further depressed by a television programme about cats, in which a vet said that it was virtually impossible to train wild cats. Although Ebenezer isn't really a wild cat but a domestic cat turned wild, we were inclined to believe him when we went to the kitchen to our own mini-tiger. For he spat and snarled as vehemently as ever, when we pleaded for his trust.

There was little we could do except to try to act as calmly and considerately towards him as possible. We began to realise that the one thing he did enjoy was milk. It had tempted him from behind the cooker, so maybe it would work again. My daughter was more courageous in approaching him than us, so she poured him a saucer of milk . . . then paused, bottle in mid-air, too astonished for words.

We were immediately immobilised, too. Nobody dared to speak a word. We all listened intently as Ebenezer voraciously lapped up his milk. Then we heard the noise that my daughter had been so surprised to hear. It was a sound like pebbles rumbling beneath a neap tide. Strong and deep, beneath his tatty fur, Ebby purred a thanks!

I felt like hugging him! Although to have done so would have been pushing my luck. But his attitide towards us soon seemed to be changing, so a little later I gingerly stroked his coat.

AFTER a preliminary wince, he permitted the familiarity, paused to study his own reactions, then, lifting his head, rubbed it against my hand.

We were all thrilled. Archimedes leaping from the bath, Columbus sighting the New World, could not have known greater satisfaction. That night, for the very first time, Ebby curled up in the bed we had prepared for him, and purred when we greeted him in the morning.

The worst was over, but he had plenty to learn.

WE tried to get him to play with a length of wool, but no-one had ever played with Ebby, and our actions puzzled him.

Warily, he studied the twitching object, then decided the whole performance was too childish for a Tom of his vast experience, and yawned.

He still spat occasionally at our approach, but it was a formal ritual, not genuine malice, and he was always ready to be caressed. In fact, once the craving for affection had been released, he couldn't be stroked enough.

By the end of a week, he was venturing out of his corner in the kitchen. Although alert, and flat eared, he was no longer constrained to the Scrooge-like sidle.

Ebby has been with us for a fortnight, now, and we still have much to teach him. Gradually, he must be escorted round the rest of the house, taught to live on terms of mutual respect with our Afghan Hound and instructed in the delights of the garden. Each lesson has to be taken in slow motion.

I soon realised the folly of trying to rush the steps in his education. For example, tired of restrictions, I took the short route to the dustbin, but opening the back door upset him so much that I have not dared to repeat the experiment.

But he'll learn in time. Of that we're confident. Every day his trust increases, and a cat's insatiable curiosity is our strongest ally.

Soon, Ebby won't be able to resist the temptation to explore the world beyond our kitchen walls. And when that day comes, we'll be there helping him, giving him confidence. For despite his wild behaviour he is a lovely cat. ■

Continued from page 29

I tried to keep out of his way. I preferred to be alone on the shore listening to the sea, which I imagined brought me whispers from across the Channel. Often I imagined I heard my father's voice comforting me, and at such times I felt very sad.

One day I was sitting about in the house, feeling very lonely, wishing that it was time for Kath to come home from work.

"Snap out of it, lad," Mrs Rudkin advised me. "Go and collect some sea coal if you're kicking your heels."

The colliery was so close to the sea that there was always coal strewn along the shore. In the back yard was an old rusting pram so I pushed it down to the shore and took my time gathering sea coal.

I'd filled the pram with coal and was about to push it back to the house so I could meet Kath off the six o'clock bus, when Billy Marvin stopped me. There were a few other children there but they wanted no part of Billy Marvin's mischief. He was bigger than the rest of us.

"What you doin' then?" Billy challenged me.

"Collecting sea coal, what do you think!" I replied.

"That's the easy way." He grinned. "Our fathers have to dig it from the ground like men."

Even then I would have passed him by, but he put his boot against the pram and blocked my way.

"What's your father doin' then, John Hemming?"

"He's away, fighting in the war!" I answered heatedly.

"So he ran off, too, like Kath Rudkin's man?" He grinned maliciously at my bewilderment.

"Kath Rudkin hasn't got a man," I said.

"Not now," he said, "he went off and left her holding the baby!" He laughed in my face.

"You're a liar, Billy Marvin!" I protested. "No man would go off and leave Kath."

His face darkened with anger, then he taunted me with insults, mostly against Kath. "You ask Kath Rudkin about her man," he ended, "the next time you're clinging to her skirts!"

Then he heaved his foot against the pram and overturned it, spilling the sea coal and scattering the other children. I'd never hit anyone in my life before that day. But I threw myself at Billy Marvin and bowled him over.

I DIDN'T have the chance to regret it. Billy Marvin wasn't only tough. He'd been taught to fight. And although the other children cheered me on, he laid into me with a vengeance. My lip was split and one eye was puffing up when someone suddenly came between us and pulled us apart.

"Billy Marvin! I hope you're ashamed of yourself."

I thought I was dreaming. Kath wasn't due home yet. But there she was holding Billy Marvin by the scruff of the neck, her face scarlet with anger.

She gave him an almighty push and he shot off across the shore like a whippet. No-one followed him.

34

CLAUDETTE COLBERT

★ ★ ★ ★ ★ ★ ★ ★ ★ ★ ★ ★ ★ ★ ★ ★ ★ ★ ★ ★

' Claudette Colbert firmly believed that the left side of her face was the better, and she refused to allow her right profile to be filmed. This sometimes required whole scenes to be rearranged around her, and cameramen who worked with her used to call her right side "the other side of the moon" — **'** because no-one ever saw it.

★ ★ ★ ★ ★ ★ ★ ★ ★ ★ ★ ★ ★ ★ ★ ★

The other children crowded round me and after that incident I was never short of a friend. After that Billy Marvin kept out of my way, too, at school and at play.

But that day, when Kath and I were alone, walking back to the house, I could hardly see for tears.

"It's all right, John," she said reassuringly. "It's over now. I'll soon have you patched up like a war hero. Billy Marvin's nothing but a bully. His whole family's the same." She paused and looked at me with concern.

"Are you in much pain, John?"

"It's . . . it's not the pain," I protested. "It was what he said Aunt Kath. About you . . ."

"Oh?" She laid her hands on both my shoulders.

"He said horrible things about you and called you names." I sobbed.

Her fingers tightened on my shoulders. "Names can't hurt anyone, John. So rest easy. You're the one who's been hurt."

IN bed that night I lay feeling sore, but pleased with myself because I'd stood up for Aunt Kath. Everyone was extra nice to me and Mrs Rudkin brought me supper on a tray. Mr Rudkin even made a joke about me looking as though I'd been in action on the Western Front. I felt happy then, especially when Kath came and sat on the edge of my bed.

"I thought you might like these to keep you company, John," she said, and put the two toby jugs on my lap. I picked them up and smiled.

"Toby jugs always look so happy, Aunt Kath. And sort of pleased with themselves."

"I know what you mean. It's just a pity that people can't be like that all the time," she said sadly. But then she seemed to force the sadness from her voice. I guessed it was for my sake. "You look pretty pleased with yourself," she told me brightly.

I didn't contradict her. I felt as though I'd championed the best cause in the world. But there was one question I couldn't stop myself asking. "Did *he* buy them for you?" I whispered.

She looked surprised. "Who?" she asked.

"The man you . . . The one who went away."

"John, pet." She reached for my hand across the bed cover. "What do you know about him?"

Without looking at her I said, "I only know that he went away to fight — and didn't come back."

She squeezed my hand then walked over to the window and looked down into the street.

"Why didn't he come back to you, Aunt Kath?"

 Filling The Gap . . .

IT really was a good play. The Man Of The House and I were quite absorbed.

Then, suddenly, there was a shrill squeak from the television set and the picture shrank to a dot — then disappeared altogether.

After much pressing of buttons and twirling of knobs, The Man Of The House threw up his hands in despair and sank into his armchair. Our evening was ruined.

Next day, the man from our local TV shop appeared, shook his head sadly and loaded our "beloved box" into his van.

"It'll take three days," he said. "At least."

That evening began like a wake. We kept glancing sadly towards that oh-so-bare corner of our living-room, afraid to look at the evening programme in case there was something really good on.

After half an hour of listening to the clock tick, I took out my work basket and The Man Of The House wandered out into the garden.

Ten minutes later, I heard the sound of the lawn mower over the hum of my sewing machine.

By bedtime, I had altered two dresses, sewn buttons on four shirts, a coat and two blouses, and The Man Of The House had the neatest garden for months.

The following evening we planned in advance. The result was: I produced three trays of home baking and The Man Of The House put long-promised shelves in the hall cupboards. We even managed a game of cards!

By the time our TV came back we wondered how we ever found the time to watch it.

We're trying not to slip back into our old ways again. I hope we don't. For we really should keep our one-eyed monster in its place. And I don't mean the corner of the living-room!

I knew the answer before she replied. Her voice was far away again like the time I'd seen her looking out of her bedroom window at the sea.

"He was killed. The very first week he was in the front line."

I didn't need to ask any more questions. My father was a soldier, like Kath's man used to be. But my father was still alive.

There were some things I didn't understand then, not for years afterwards. I was just a boy. But it was like being in a church just then.

Aunt Kath turned away from the window and the setting sun was like golden fire in her hair. She might have had a halo round her head the way I felt about her.

"I'm here, Aunt Kath." I said in my champion's voice. "I'll always look after you."

"Will you, my laddie?"

She looked at me for a long moment, then smiled. "Yes," she said, "I think you will."

"Oh, I will," I insisted, wanting to convince her.

"I told you once not to be in a hurry to grow up, John," she said. "But grow up you will. And one day you'll meet the right woman. And she'll be a fine woman too."

She went out of the room, leaving me with the toby jugs. Their faces were smiling as ever, but somehow, in that moment, they seemed sad, too.

I got out of bed and tiptoed across the landing to Kath's room. It was empty. I put the toby jugs back on her dressing-table. And I never touched them again . . .

WHEN the war ended, I was reluctant to leave the little mining village. But the evacuation authorities arranged for me to go back to London, for my father was coming home . . .

I was overjoyed to be reunited with him and a new life began for us together.

Just before Aunt Kath's birthday I asked if he would buy me a toby jug. At that time my father would have bought me anything I asked for. Toby jugs weren't easy to get but he managed to find me one — a plump little fellow in a red coat, with a familiar smile.

Together we wrapped up the toby jug so that it wouldn't break in the post and we sent it off in time for Kath's birthday. With it, Dad sent a long letter thanking Kath for all she'd done for me, as well as a letter to Mr and Mrs Rudkin thanking them for looking after me.

In return, we had a letter from Kath thanking us for the toby jug. She also invited us to go up and see the family some time.

Dad accepted the invitation gratefully. He wanted to be able to see the home where I'd been able to take sanctuary during the troubled years when he was away. And I felt I would burst with happiness at the thought of seeing Kath again.

Kath was shy and reserved when she first met my father. But like the rest of the Rudkins, she took to him. Before we left the village she promised one day she'd come and visit us.

It was only when Kath came down to London and stayed a

weekend with us, I began to realise what was happening. Of course, my father wouldn't rush into anything.

He'd been a widower too long not to have doubts and uncertainties. But he and Kath visited each other every few weeks, and wrote long letters between visits.

They became engaged the following Christmas. My contribution to the proceedings was another toby jug. This time I gave it by hand to Kath and she burst into tears. I thought I'd upset her until she put her arm around me taking my breath clean away.

"It's beautiful, John," she said tenderly, stroking the toby jug.

A little embarrassed, with her and my father watching me, I stammered, "But will you mind being my mother, Aunt Kath?"

"Mind?" Her laughter echoed my father's. Then solemnly she told me:

"You'll be like the child I should have had."

At first I looked to my father, but he understood. And I remembered the time when Kath had been ill and realised that she'd lost her baby. Now I was old enough to understand. And I was glad.

My father married Kath in the spring and we all lived together in London close to Dad's work. For the first time in my life, I knew real, complete happiness.

Happiness seemed to make the years fly away. I grew up, I grew away from my parents. First university, then a job far away in North Wales. But Kath was always with me in my heart.

And her words came true. I met the right girl, and we married. And we called our first daughter Kathleen.

We moved around the country and sometimes lived abroad. But no matter where we were, I always sent my mother a toby jug on her birthday.

At the last count she had over 30, some were more valuable than others but to her they were all equally precious. More than one dealer has offered her a pretty sum for them.

But money could never buy them. For I can never forget the time when Kath, lonely and distressed, had whispered more to herself than to me:

"The toby jugs were to be the start of a collection. A special collection to go on and on over the years . . ."

★   ★   ★   ★

I looked up at my daughter and smiled.

She glanced down at the toby jug nestling in her hands, then she turned to me.

"Can I wrap it up, Dad?" she asked.

I looked across at Mary still standing by the door.

"Yes, Kath," I said. "Of course you can."

She put the toby jug back in the box and reached for the wrapping paper.

"So, in a way, her soldier did come home to her after all . . ." she said.

"Yes," I replied. "He did, didn't he . . . ?"

———————— * THE END * ————————

THERE'S NO GOING BACK...

Caught in the biggest crisis of her life, it was a message from a complete stranger that pointed the way ahead . . .

Complete Story by MARGARET FOX

THE train was just slowing down when the woman in the opposite seat spoke. "Would you like a cup of tea, love? What do you say to me getting both of us a cup, eh? There's a place down the corridor where you can get them. A sort of buffet."

Mary looked up to see a short, plump, elderly woman — the owner of the kind voice. Mary tried to smile, and if the attempt was heroic it lacked, above all things, conviction. But it was too late anyway, for the woman had seen that she'd been crying. She had been sitting, half-turned, staring out of the window, hoping nobody would notice, but they had. At least this woman had . . .

The train had stopped now and the schoolgirl with the violin case and the boy with the transistor got out. They were alone, Mary and the kind-faced woman.

"Thank you," said Mary. "It would be nice but shall I . . ."

"No, love. You just stay where you are. I know my legs aren't what they once were, but I can manage all right."

That left Mary alone. Though she had her thoughts — thoughts about how the day had been a complete failure. Of course it had, she might have known that it would be. Pilgrimages into the past always were, she supposed. It was all so cliched. Couldn't she have guessed that the field where she used to play was now a housing estate? Couldn't she have visualised tiny little red brick houses covering the field where once they'd gathered buttercups and wild purply geraniums?

Oh, don't let me cry again. Please, don't let me cry . . .

The woman came back. She had a plastic beaker in each hand and, as she handed one to Mary, she spilled some tea on the floor.

"Oh, well, as long as it didn't go on that nice suit of yours. Have you got any aspirins?"

"No, no, I don't think so, but I'm quite all right. Honestly, I am. Please, don't bother any more."

"Well, I have, so here, take a couple. And don't think I'm pushing in because I'm not, but I daresay with the tea they might help a bit."

"Thank you," said Mary again. "You're very kind."

FUNNY how people are kind, like Miss Marsden. Miss Marsden had kept the village shop where once Mary had bought her sweets and fetched things for her mother. Old Miss Marsden had always known what you wanted before you asked for it. If she knew you were having guests she had extra bread and eggs waiting for you without them being ordered . . .

But now Miss Marsden was dead. Oh, her shop was still there, but instead of rows upon rows of jars and barrels of tea there were tins, and notices that said, *Three pence off your next purchase*. And, of course, nobody spoke to her, indeed nobody even knew her name.

She'd thought it would be a good thing for the children to be brought up in the country. But now she knew she hadn't been thinking about the children at all, that the main reason had lain within her own self. She'd wanted to go back to the place where she'd been happy, because now she was so desperately, desperately unhappy.

The loneliness since Tony had left her had been unbearable — and

SHIRLEY TEMPLE

★ ★ ★ ★ ★ ★ ★ ★ ★ ★ ★ ★ ★

‘ "I stopped believing in Santa Claus at an early age. Mother took me to see him in a Hollywood department store and he asked me for my autograph." ’

★ ★ ★ ★ ★ ★ ★ ★ ★ ★ ★ ★ ★

it hadn't got any better. It had just mounted up and up, engulfing her, threatening to destroy her . . .

FEELING any better now?" the kindly woman asked.
"Yes, thank you," Mary lied, "much better." Well at any rate she wasn't crying any more. As she sipped on her tea she remembered how she'd gone to the village church and there was a new vicar she'd never heard of.

But the worst thing had been going back to the house where she had spent her childhood. She'd thought that there, at least, nothing would have changed. But it had — the garden had shrunk to a slit because of road widening and a hand-painted board had read — *Bed and Breakfast.*

The train was slowing down again and then it shuddered to a halt. It was silent then, as if the train was resting between breaths.

"It always does this here," the woman said. "Goodness knows why . . . Anyway, I'm getting out at the next station, so it gives me time to collect my bits and pieces. You going on to St Pancras?"

"Yes. I've been spending the day in the village where I was a child."

"Oh, changed a bit, has it?"

"Yes."

"Thought it would have," said the woman.

Mary had not been able to believe it when Tony said he was leaving them, that he cared for somebody else. She'd been stunned, confused. It had been a time when she hadn't been able to think about what she was going to do. That was when life had become a nightmare. Then her only consolation had been that one day she would wake up, and everything would be fine again. That none of it had really happened, that Tony still loved her . . .

Waking had come under a different guise called realisation. And at that the pain increased, until she was afraid she would crack. She *was* cracking; she was taking it out on the children. She had to do something. Anything. That was why today she tried to find somewhere to hide, somewhere to run to . . .

"Well, this is where I leave you." The woman was now lumbering to her feet, and her round red face was lit with wonderful kindness. "So you just keep on, love, and things will improve. I don't know what's gone wrong. And, no doubt, even if there was time I wouldn't want you to tell me. But let me tell you this. There's no going back in this world, you know. But there's always something round the corner, so just you be ready for it, that's my advice . . ."

"Now where did I put those cooking apples? Oh, there they are and my ticket's inside my glove so that's all right . . . Take care of yourself."

Then in a flurry she was gone and the train went on to St Pancras. Mary knew that her children, Jean and Richard, would be waiting for her at home.

Jeremy Lumb, the artist from across the road, had said he would

Morning Has Broken . . .

WHAT kind of "morning person" are you? The reason I ask is that, the other day, the subject came up when a few friends were round for coffee.

Having compared notes, we came to the conclusion that there's a lot of the Jekyll and Hyde in all of us — certainly for that first hour of a new day.

For how we behave in that time seems to bear no relationship to our normal personalities.

It seems the most easy going of people can be real grouches in the morning.

Here are some of the types that came to light.

The Silent Slouch. Very common, this one. Invariably wears aged dressing-gown and slippers. Never hurries. Can put up with anything except conversation and cooked breakfasts.

The Washing Warbler. Whistles from the minute feet touch the floor. Particularly enjoys the acoustics of the bathroom. Always emerges with bright eyes and a hearty appetite. Creates havoc if married to a Silent Slouch.

The Radio Raver. Plays Radio One at full volume. Known to hold one-sided conversations because no-one can hear what's being said.

The Breakfast-time Bear (with a sore head). This one will converse but only in short, sharp growls, usually from behind a newspaper, and only to point out that the toast is burnt.

Well, come on — do you recognise yourself?
I certainly do, but I'm not saying.
Well, some things are sacred!

call in to see that everything was OK but Mary knew they would be all right. Jean was older and more practical than Richard but they were both quite capable of looking after themselves. For a while anyway . . .

St Pancras came, and she was lost in the stream of people as they jostled to get away. Outside the station she got a bus to Charing Cross and then caught another train that took her to the southern suburb where they lived. She was tired. No, it was more than that, for she'd gone beyond the stage of just plain tiredness. Now it was as if, somewhere, her mechanism had missed a beat and the natural rhythm of living had been by-passed. Then, of course, there was the thinking, too, the almost compulsive thinking out of what tomorrow would bring. Tomorrow . . .

By the time she reached her own street it was dark. There was a light in Jeremy's studio, and she knew that he would be working, getting ready for his one-man show. She hoped it would be a success. He was kind, he deserved success . . .

Opposite, in her own home, the children had left lights on everywhere, but most of the rooms would be empty. She opened the door and went in.

HELLO, darlings," she called, trying hard to keep the weariness out of her voice. "Where are you? Are you famished?"

They came into the hall but they didn't rush up to her as she'd expected, as she had hoped. Instead they stood very close together and she realised they were afraid.

"I suppose we're going back to where you lived when you were a little girl, then," said Jean.

"It's where you've been all day, isn't it?"

Her fear was making her sound truculent, almost rude.

"No." She smiled at them and although her jaws ached with the effort and her eyes burned, somehow she managed to show them her love. "No, we're not going back. We're staying here," she said quietly. "There's nowhere to go back to. Perhaps there never is. I made a mistake."

They only partly understood, of course. They didn't know there was anything else to understand, but they began jumping up and down. They were happy again.

"We're staying here, we're staying here, we're staying here," they chanted.

"And I can go on the trip with the school, can't I?" Jean said. "I've decided to go in for biology, too. Do you think it's a good idea? Say you do, Mum."

"And I can go in for the junior essay prize," Richard said hesitantly, smiling his shy, attractive smile. "Mr Barton says I'm very imaginative and that I've got a good chance. Are you pleased?"

"Yes, darling, very pleased."

Continued on page 48

43

The COTTINGLEY FAIRIES Mystery

By BETTY PUTTICK

DO you believe in fairies?" Peter Pan asks children every Christmas.

And every Christmas they shout back that they do.

But away from J. M. Barrie's enchanted world, ask someone if they believe in fairies, and you get rather a funny look!

It was much the same many years ago when Elsie Wright first talked about the fairies in the garden behind her parents' cottage in the Yorkshire village of Cottingley.

In July 1917, Elsie's South African cousin, Frances Griffiths, was staying with her mother at the Wrights' home while her father was at the war.

That summer Elsie was sixteen, and Frances nine. The girls often mentioned seeing fairies when they played in the glen, and this brought some good-natured teasing from the grown-ups.

Elsie could bear it no longer.

"Look here, Father, if you'll let us have your camera and tell me how it works, I'll get a photo of the fairies," she promised.

Mr Wright wasn't keen on this idea. He had recently acquired a

The two young girls had stunned the whole country with their photographs of fairies. When you have read this fascinating account of their story — published some years ago — we will then disclose the final truth . . .

small camera, and he enjoyed taking snaps and developing them himself using the scullery cupboard as a darkroom.

He was afraid the girls might spoil his pleasure but they pestered him until he showed Elsie how the camera worked.

He was working in the garden when the two excited girls came back an hour later.

"We've got the photo, I believe," Elsie said. "Will you look?"

But Mr Wright was busy then, and it wasn't until evening that he began to develop the plate, with Elsie squashed into the scullery cupboard beside him. Both could see dark figures appearing, which puzzled Mr Wright, who thought they looked rather like swans, but Elsie called excitedly to Frances.

"We've got them, you'll see!"

Next morning, when Mr Wright took a print, he stared, amazed, at the now-famous picture of Frances and a group of dancing fairies.

Like many people who've seen it since, his first impression was that the girls had faked it. But they insisted they had simply photographed the fairies they talked about so often, and no questioning could shake their story.

The girls were usually truthful, but the Wrights were not entirely convinced this time. Perhaps they had used cut-out fairy figures?

While Elsie and Frances were elsewhere, Mr Wright made a thorough search of the glen round the waterfall where the picture was taken, to see if he could find any tell-tale scraps of paper.

The Wrights also searched the girls' bedroom, but found nothing suspicious anywhere.

A month later, the girls borrowed the camera again, and produced a picture of Elsie with a gnome. This was not so clear as the first one, and the girls said the gnome had leaped up just as Frances snapped the shutter.

Still suspecting a childish prank, the Wrights let the mystery drop soon after this, and the photographic plates and prints were put away.

THAT night might have been the end of the story, but three years later Mrs Wright happened to attend a lecture where fairies were mentioned. She asked the speaker "If he thought fairies were really true," and later showed him the fairy photographs. He sent them to Edward Gardner, a psychic investigator.

Like the Wrights, Mr Gardner thought the pictures must have been doctored in some way, and asked if he could see the negatives. He took these to a professional photographer, a Mr Snelling, who examined the quarter plate glass negatives for a long time.

His comments on the picture of Frances and the fairies were surprising.

"This plate is a single exposure," he reported. "These dancing figures are not made of paper, nor of any fabric. They are not painted on a photographed background. But what gets me most is that all these figures have moved during exposure."

Later, after enlarging the pictures for closer examination, his verdict was that they were "entirely genuine unfaked photographs of single exposure open air work."

He went on to declare that they show movement in all the fairy figures, and there is no trace whatever of studio work involving card or paper models, dark backgrounds, painted figures, etc.

"In my opinion, they are both straight, untouched pictures," he finished.

Further developments soon followed. Sir Arthur Conan Doyle, the creator of Sherlock Holmes, was interested by the tale when it reached his ears. He was preparing an article on fairies for the Christmas issue of the "Strand" magazine and felt the Cottingley pictures could provide ideal illustrations.

But before using them, he and Mr Gardner decided to consult Kodak about their authenticity.

The men were told that although there was no sign of faked work, Kodak could not certify that the pictures were genuine, as "photography lent itself to a multitude of processes, and some clever operator might have made them artificially."

The studio chief suggested that a photograph could have been taken of Frances in the glen, then the fairy figures painted on to an enlarged print, and re-photographed. But he admitted it would be skilful work, and take some time.

That was when Mr Gardner decided to visit Cottingley, and meet the Wrights for himself.

THEY were a cheerful, forthright Yorkshire couple, obviously surprised by the expert's opinions of the photographs.

Elsie, a shy, pretty girl, took him to see the glen, and he was impressed to find that some extra-large toadstools, which had seemed almost too appropriate in the picture, were actually growing by the stream.

Edward Gardner decided to ask the girls to try for further photographs that summer, and evolved a plan to foil any chances of deception.

Elsie's cousin, Frances, returned to Cottingley from her new home in Scarborough, and in August 1920, Gardner gave the girls a camera each, and two dozen plates which had been secretly marked at the factory.

He then went away, leaving the girls to "'tice the fairies," as they called it, and get any photographs they could. He felt that if he stayed, too, nothing would happen.

The next fortnight was wet, and the girls could only visit the glen during two sunny spells.

Elsie sent Mr Gardner three negatives from the marked batch. There was a picture of each girl with a fairy, and a mysterious third photograph showing misty faces and figures entangled in the harebells and grass of the undergrowth, which experts described as "impossible to fake."

All three prints were greatly enlarged and minutely examined for fake or trickery, again without result.

The Christmas 1920 issue of the "Strand" magazine with the article entitled *An Epoch-Making Event — Fairies Photographed by Conan Doyle and Edward Gardner*, caused great interest.

THE next year, Mr Gardner asked a medium, Geoffrey Hodson, to assess the girls' clairvoyant powers. Mr Hodson went to the glen with Elsie and Frances, where "he saw all they say, and more." He found the glen and stream "swarming with many forms of elemental life," like gnomes, fairies, elves and brownies.

But there were no photographs this time. According to Mr Gardner, the fairy forms were not sufficiently dense to photograph, and any attempt made them retreat. Conan Doyle suggested in his book, *The Coming Of The Fairies*, that although both girls were sufficiently clairvoyant to see the fairies, puberty had diminished Frances' powers as a medium.

Yet, it came to light that Elsie was good at painting and drawing at school, and she did work for a time in a photographer's studio.

What was Elsie really saying when in 1971, she was asked how it had all been done? "I've told you that they're photographs of figments of our imagination, and that's what I'm sticking to."

What, then, is the truth about the Cottingley Fairies?

The Fairy Bower.

FRESH light on this long-lasting mystery was shed in 1982/3 when the editor of the British Journal of Photography recounted the Cottingley story, and gave his own technical explanation of how the famous fairy pictures could have been produced.

In April 1983 he published a letter from Elsie confirming that the pictures were a "practical joke which fell flat on its face." Her cousin Frances, then nine years old, was scolded by her mother for getting wet in the stream at Cottingley Dell, and her explanation that she had been playing with the fairies did not calm the situation!

It was Elsie's idea to "prove" to the sceptical grown-ups that there were fairies in the dell, by photographing some created from cardboard cut-outs and hat-pins, then the joke would be on them when the girls revealed their hoax.

But when Sir Arthur Conan Doyle became involved, and there was so much publicity, it became impossible to admit the truth. Their secret was to last most of their long lives.

In an interview a few years ago, Frances, while agreeing with Elsie's

Continued overleaf

Continued from previous page

story, claimed that there had been real fairies in the dell, as one photograph titled "Fairy Bower" showed.

When Frances died in 1986, her daughter said, "She never changed her story. She could not tell a lie if she tried." She went on to say that her mother had often seen fairies — the last time during the second World War as she stood by her kitchen sink.

On hearing this, Elsie still asserted that the Fairy Bower picture was, like the others, part of their childish hoax. "The joke" she said, "was to last two hours, and it has lasted seventy years."

Now Elsie, too, has gone. She died in June 1988. So what was the real truth about Cottingley Dell?

It's my guess that the famous Cottingley Fairy story will always retain that element of mystery. Who is to say which sister's version is the true one? It has been said that Frances had clairvoyant qualities which Elsie did not — so could they *both* be right — according to their own experiences?

Continued from page 43

And she had nearly dragged them back, nearly ruined things for them. But she had been saved. Just in time, she thought.

Gratitude, something she'd not known since Tony left, flowed gently over her.

"Has Mr Lumb been in?" she asked, trying to sound ordinary and casual.

"Yes, we played dominoes, and he says we've to call him Jeremy. And I said I would wave when you got safely back, but I nearly forgot. He seemed worried about you . . ."

Jean rushed off and pulled back the curtains in the sitting-room.

"Is he keen on you?" she called over her shoulder.

Mary laughed.

"We'll ask him for supper one evening soon if you like. But now, as it's a special occasion, we'll open that tin of chicken," she said to Richard.

"But on special occasions we have flowers and candles and crackers and the best cups and things. We're only in the kitchen."

"Nevertheless this is a special occasion all the same, a *very* special one. You see, I've learnt something. An old woman with a bag of apples in the train taught me."

Richard laughed delightedly.

"You're pretending. It's a fairy story."

"No, I'm not," she said. It's true. Terribly true."

She knew now that a long road lay in front of her. Knew that there would be days that would be cruel to endure. She had no illusions, but after today she knew which way to face — forward. She was going to be ready for what was round the bend. Ready for happiness again if it should ever come to her . . .

——————— * **THE END** * ———————

L-PLATES FOR LOVE

**The driving lessons were for someone else's
girl. At least, that's how it all started . . .**

THE man came into the garage just as I was thinking of going back
— I nearly said home — to my bachelor flat in the cheap part
of town.

The garage was a joint venture. Iles and I had always been mad
about cars and when we left school we served our apprenticeships
together at an enormous garage where the showroom sported a
carpet.

Then we'd borrowed and scraped up a down-payment together and
went in for a couple of ramshackle sheds and two petrol pumps. We
made enough to eat but not to play.

So last year I went on this Advanced Motoring Course. When I got back we bought a big broom cupboard at a jumble sale and stuck it in the corner of the biggest shed for an office. Then we plastered the local Press with adverts for driving tuition . . .

It helped a bit, but during slack times I still climbed into my overalls and got underneath various old cars. Some days it felt like a Jekyll and Hyde existence — one minute smart suit, white shirt, tie and consoling manner; next greasy overalls and spanners.

So when this man came in I was glad I'd just changed to go home and looked like a driving instructor.

"Mr Iles?" he said.

"No, I'm Alan Crawford. Mr Iles has taken a client for a test run. How can I help you, sir?"

"I'm really after driving lessons and I saw your advertisement in the paper —"

"That's me. I'm the instructing half of the team." I gave him my most reassuring smile.

He was one of those thin, anxious types who consider all things mechanical as their natural enemies. My heart sank as he slipped in a pool of oil and clutched my arm like a drowning man.

"So sorry —" He was breathing heavily as if he'd been running. "Not myself —"

"Come and sit down, sir." I led him to a pile of tyres and got him safely wedged in the top of one. "A lot of people — like yourself — want driving lessons after office hours."

"Oh, it's not for myself, Mr Crawford." He paused and took another lungful of air. "For my girlfriend."

I WAS thankful he wasn't going to be my pupil. Either he was out of condition or suffering from some nervous trouble.

"Glad you feel you can put your trust in our tuition, sir," I said smoothly. "Will it be an evening appointment or — ?"

"She's waiting outside St James's Church now!" He gasped. "I told her to sit by the fountain and not to move until I got back."

He paused and held his side. "I read your advert while we waited for the breakdown truck. And I ran most of the way here —"

"Your car broke down?" I prompted, beginning to see more than one snag.

"You could say that. Pamela tried to drive it through that pedestrian way at the side of the fountain, and it stopped at the first bollard."

"Pamela — ?"

"My girlfriend." He looked gloomy. "At least she was. I've been teaching her to drive."

I was beginning to see daylight. "It's not always a good idea to teach someone close to you," I said, trotting out all the psychology patter. "Possibly Miss — ?"

"Miss Withers," he supplied.

"Possibly Miss Withers does not take kindly to your — er — advice."

"She completely ignores it. I shouted, 'Brake!' and she jumped on the accelerator. The next minute we're halfway round this concrete bollard. My car's only two years old.

"And we could have injured someone," he added as a bit of an afterthought.

"The police — ?"

"Very understanding. She has a way with her — I'll give her that. She'll have to pay for the damage, of course."

He didn't say, "We'll have to pay." A real gent, I thought.

"If you're feeling better now, shall we go into the office and sort out a suitable time? You needn't have run here, you know. We are on the telephone."

He stood up. "She didn't have another ten pence. Besides —" He dusted off the seat of his trousers. "Besides, she refused to consider any further lessons."

He went on, not meeting my eye. "She's had a go with the City Driving School and the U-Drive Tuition people. And now me," he finished lamely.

"I see," I said grimly. "Then probably she's right to give up any idea of driving. There's such a thing as a non-driver, you know, sir."

"Rubbish," he said stoutly. "Anyone can drive a car. She promised

---

DO AS I SAY

I go out to an evening class on Monday nights, and one evening I had coffee with a friend afterwards and arrived home about eleven o'clock.

To my amazement there was panic in the household. The garage doors were open and my husband's car gone, and at the hall door stood our seventeen-year-old son, peering out into the darkness.

"Where on earth have you been, Mum?" was his greeting. "You're very late. Dad's gone out to look for you!"

A few minutes later he arrived back in his car, all hot and bothered, and quite annoyed with me for being so late.

I was secretly rather flattered at all the attention my extra hour had caused. I didn't even bother to remind both of them of all the evenings I have worried over them when they've been really late home.

After all, I'm sure the rules are different for mums!

---

me she'd learn so that she could give me a hand with my deliveries — Clarkson's Delicatessen." He mentioned it casually, then looked up to see if I was suitably impressed.

It was one of those newly-opened gourmet places that made our small town feel all cosmopolitan. Right then it made me feel warm towards things like fish and chips, sausage and mash. And much warmer towards Miss Pamela Withers . . .

So I didn't tell him that, though Ken and I were after business, we weren't in the habit of taking the City School's drop-outs. Instead I sighed deeply and reached for the appointment book.

"Er — hum!" He was clearing his throat behind me. "I did wonder — as you're not actually out on a job at the moment — I mean, you

Continued on page 54

"Watch Your Language!"

At home, in Britain, it was "Viva Espāna" all the way for Anna Kirwan. But as soon as she set foot on Spanish soil, she found herself speechless . . .

WHOEVER it was that said "a little learning is a dangerous thing," warning us to "drink deep or not at all," knew what he was talking about. And I'm convinced it was Spanish he had in mind when he wrote those immortal words. It's just a pity I didn't take his advice.

As soon as our holiday to Spain was booked, I foolishly enrolled for a crash course to learn the language.

The class was full of love-sick girls, all dreaming of a boy they'd left behind in Majorca, Torremolinos — you name it and watch their eyes blur up with memories.

Memories of a boy with eyes dark as treacle who swore that part of his heart was broken for ever when she went away. And, what's more, he swore it in English.

The fact that he's learned this sentence off pat for each fond farewell makes no difference. It works every time and accounts for all those girls queueing up to learn the language of their Don Juan.

IT was Ibiza. I was just nipping over the road to a chemist's shop, when I was startled out of my bikini by a piercing whistle from the policeman on point duty.

Holding up the whole town with one wave of his hand, he demanded to know:

"Que significa esto?"

"It signifies, señor," I replied in dictionary Spanish, "that I'm pinching over the chemist and if we weren't spending weather in this mode, crooking words, I could be

there in a spasm."

Get the drift? No, neither did he. And we would still be there bandying words, if my John hadn't come along with a few well-chosen gestures and sorted us out.

Of course, gestures are what I should have studied in the first place. Gestures get him everywhere.

And Spanish gestures are so many and so remarkable that one day I'll compile a dictionary of them instead of words.

Words just don't get you anywhere. Take the time I tried to help an elderly English woman in difficulties with a railway official.

They were at it hammer and tongs, but not communicating at all. So with a few well-chosen words, I enquired what was wrong, and the poor soul grabbed at me.

Cockney batterd my right ear, while Spanish machine-gunned my right. Between the two I eventually learned the unfortunate woman had lost her purse.

"It isn't so much the money, ducks," she told me, "but it had a photo of me poor 'usband in it."

"Leave it to me," I told her, and informed the official that she'd just lost her football team.

Naturally, there was a crowd round us by this time and, with a broad wink at his audience, the Spaniard enquired whether it was Real Madrid or Manchester United.

The crowd loved it and, amid gales of Spanish laughter, I went on to describe the missing bag as "dark green with two sleeves" and, pointing to the unfortunate woman: "It belongs to *him*."

The official drew himself up; a policeman with a revolver at his hip swung over and told me that I was causing a disturbance, and would I either move on or go to jail.

We broke up instantly, before we were taken into custody.

WELL, it's your own fault," John my nearest and dearest, said. "Should have let them stew in . . . "

Stew! We suddenly felt hungry.

"Right," Hubby said, steering me into the nearest café. "Now you can do your stuff, get us some eats."

I studied the menu carefully and got my speech prepared. Then came my big moment.

"Fish and Fried Paws," I ordered.

The waiter's face was a study in control. The liar had just told me that my Spanish was "estupendo," and quite carried away, I forgot that *papas* was potatoes while *patas* was paws.

"Patas, señora?"

"Si, si," I said briskly, and went on to order two glasses of blood!

The waiter struggled with his face.

"Chips, she means," John piped up. "You know, to go with bangers, washed down with some red plonk with stuff floating about."

"Fool," I hissed. "You surely don't expect him to understand that!"

But he did. The rotten waiter understood every word.

"Thought you could speak Spanish." John smirked.

And for once, I didn't mince words — in my very best Spanish, of course! ∎

Continued from page 51
know what they say about getting on a horse immediately after
you've had a fall . . ."

MISS WITHERS was waiting on the seat just as Clarkson had
said. She was gazing at the bollard she'd so recently messed
up, which couldn't have been good for her confidence.

I'd expected someone on the loud side, used to battling with
Clarkson, argumentative, a flashy smile. But she wasn't like that.

A knitted cap kept her fair hair off her pale oval face. Her eyes
were big and apprehensive and her full mouth trembled a little as
Clarkson introduced us.

I shook her hand and gave her my full-beam, reassuring smile.
Clarkson had her right under his thumb, it was pathetic.

He was all benevolence now. "Alan thought it best if you drove
again as soon as possible, Pamela. It's nice and quiet through the
town and back to Poplar Avenue."

So it was my idea now! And christian names all round!

"Charles, I told you, I can't face it again. I just want to go home."

"Pamela —"

Even I could hear the warning bite in his voice. "Look, Miss
Withers," I said quickly, "I wouldn't dream of asking you to drive
through the streets after your recent — er — accident. I thought of
going to an old airfield — it's past the Poplar Estate so we could
drop Mr Clarkson off on our way —"

A look of satisfaction crept into his face and I realised that had
been the idea all along. A free lift back home — doubtless she'd have
to pay for the lesson — how low could anyone get!

"We could have a gentle cruise around the runway," I went on,
"just to get the feel of the controls again . . ." I widened my smile
and tried to put sincerity, integrity and sheer lovability into my gaze.

It seemed to work. Her lower lip stopped shaking and lengthened
into the beginning of an answering smile.

"Oh, all right, if you really think it's worth it. It's good of you to
come out now at such short notice. I'm afraid I've got a sort of block
when it comes to driving, but as you're so kind —"

During all this I was getting her into the car before she could
change her mind. It wasn't a bit cold but I got a rug out of the boot
and tucked it over her knees and adjusted the head-rest. I wanted to
fuss over her. Only because of Clarkson's manner, of course.

He got into the back with ill-grace and immediately I drove off.

"Don't see each other until the test is over," I said calmly.

Pamela drew in her breath quickly but said nothing. Clarkson
hummed and hawed in amazement.

"It sounds unreasonable, I know," I swept on, trying to look
confident, "but it's obvious to me, an outsider, that you are both
under considerable strain. This whole thing is, shall we say, driving a
wedge between you which may permanently damage your future
relationships."

I looked at Pamela. She wouldn't return my gaze nor look round at Clarkson, but she nodded once.

"Right!" I said briskly, as if I did this kind of deal every day. "The sooner we start."

Clarkson scrambled out as I started the engine. Then he poked his head through Pamela's window.

"Farewell then, darling," he said dramatically, trying to make it all a big laugh. "In five weeks' time, a new woman!"

He pecked a kiss on her cheek and I put the car into gear and moved quickly off, hoping to decapitate him.

WE didn't speak a word till we got to the airfield. Pamela's pale face was flushed, her teeth nibbling her lower lip. I got out and went round to her side.

"Anywhere you like. Any speed you like. Just drive," I said.

She looked up at me, debating whether to mutiny. Then she slid over into the driver's seat, clonked into first and started away with a kangaroo jump that made my jawbone ache.

"Fine," I said gaily as we continued in a series of bounds. "Change into second whenever you like."

She did so and we settled down to a grinding eight miles an hour. Then she managed third, except that we slewed violently to the right. And at last, when we reached a speed of 25, she made it into fourth, wrenching the wheel to the left.

We faltered along, sometimes on the runway, sometimes off. She was like one of the fake films of racing drivers; her hands on the wheel kept up a continual pendulum swing. She just didn't even seem to be able to hold the thing still.

I began to hum a tune. It was obvious to me that Pamela Withers was a classic non-driver. In five weeks' time she'd fail her test and that would be the end of her so-called romance with Clarkson.

I would console her, look after her, be around to drive her wherever she wanted to go. So business would drop off still more. Who cared? I couldn't imagine a better way of spending my time.

I beamed at her as I asked her to slow down and stop. We ran into

Continued overleaf

Songs Learned At My Mother's Knee

There were few nursery rhymes and soothing lullabies in my childhood, says Sheila Byrne. No — the hand that rocked my cradle had much more interesting musical tastes . . .

I'M told that once, at a Sunday school concert, I startled the audience by singing a song that contained the unforgettable lines:

"But now he's left me and he's gone to sea,
"That great big man-o'-war from out o' the breweree."

I don't remember that incident, but I can well believe it, because the songs my mother taught me were not the nursery rhymes most children learned at their mother's knee. And I don't know where she ever learned them!

Mother's repertoire was composed of a selection of what we must charitably assume were music-hall ditties, although Mother swore she was never in a music-hall in her life.

Whatever the truth, she had a song for every occasion. She was extremely vocal on the subject of faithful and unfaithful lovers, girls who were jilted at church doors and hearts that clung like the ivy. Her babies were lulled to sleep to the stirring strains of:

"If I'd a wife and she got tight, I know what I would do,
"I'd buy her a boat and set her afloat and paddle my own canoe."

I suspect Mother's renderings weren't always accurate, but I doubt if they lost anything by that. But was there ever really a song that went:

"Dear little girly-girly, her hair is so curly-curly,
"And every morning early, I go my girl to see,
"Her teeth they are pearly-pearly, everything's whirly-whirly,
"Without my girly-girly, what would the wide world be?"

Certainly I'll never forget her rendition of "Bridget Reilly." It began:

"Arrah, Wake up, Bridget Reilly, and jump out of bed,
"Open your window and throw out your head,
"Fly with me now, to regions afar,
"If you won't do that you may stay as you are."

MOTHER was never further afield than the seaside for a few weeks' holidays, yet she had in her repertoire some tunes so

Continued from previous page

some long grass. She switched off the engine.

"First lesson over. Quite painless, wasn't it?" I said happily.

She looked at her hands as they rested on the wheel. They were small hands with tapering fingers. No engagement ring in sight.

"I'm not going to make it, am I?" she said tightly. "It's the steering, you see. I know I grind the gears and that sort of thing, but I get over that after a bit. I just can't steer straight."

"You'll be all right," I said. "You need confidence, that's all."

She didn't say anything. After a bit I added gently, "It isn't the most important thing in the world, you know, to drive a car."

I was surprised at her reaction. She looked up at me, and gazed

nostalgic they'd make you think she'd spent her life in exile. One I particularly loved was called "When The Fields Are White With Daisies." Some of you may remember it:

"When the fields are white with daisies, and the roses bloom again,

"And the lovelight in your eyes is as of yore,

"When I'm your sweetheart only, and remember when you're lonely,

"When the fields are white with daisies, I'll return."

Another song of exile had a very plaintive ring:

"As I watch the swallows on their homeward way, speeding o'er the western foam,

"Fain would I be flying, for oh! my heart is sighing, longing for that dear old home.

"For I long to see my dear old home again, the cottage by the little winding lane,

"I can see the roses climbing and hear the old bells chiming, and I'm longing for that dear old home."

Mother never sighed for long, though. She would soon revert to her customary disreputable ditties and announce resoundingly that "George Took Her Walking In The Park" or that "All The Nice Girls Love A Sailor."

Mother was nearly eighty when she died but her tastes in music never changed. One of my last recollections of her was seeing her on her knees in the garden, weeding a flower bed and singing contentedly at the top of her voice:

"Come, come, come and make eyes at me,

"Down at the old Bull and Bush . . ." ∎

right into my eyes. "It's the most important thing to me, Alan. I've got to pass that test. Will you help me?"

I was absolutely flabbergasted. That look had been like a pledge. It said a million things — that she was feeling the same as me; that love at first sight was true after all; that life was wonderful — full of promise — all that sort of thing. Then she as good as asked me to deliver her into that Clarkson's arms, neatly wrapped and tied, in five weeks' time.

Somehow I cleared my head, then my throat, then I said — well, what else could I say? — "Of course I'll help you, Pamela."

The next evening Pamela drove worse than ever and all that week

Continued overleaf

Continued from previous page

she was the same. I'd made up my mind not to talk about anything except cars and driving, but I had to loosen her up, try to find some way to help her. So one night I stopped for fish and chips and we ate them in the car and talked.

14 and her sister was training as a nurse and couldn't make a home for her. She went to live with old Mrs Clarkson, who had been her mother's best friend. Charles, 10 years older than she was, had kept her busy running errands round the shop.

It became the accepted thing that they would marry later on. Mrs Clarkson was thrilled but Charles let her know now and then he was doing her a big favour.

He didn't like it when she refused to join him in the shop and took a job in a day nursery. He didn't like it when she moved out of the Clarkson house and into her sister and new brother-in-law's flat. But the final straw was when she wrapped his two-year-old car around the bollard outside St James's Church.

"If I don't pass the test, we're finished," she concluded a few days later. Because once we'd begun eating fish and chips and talking, we couldn't stop and all this information took nearly a week to get.

Well, there it was again in case I'd had any doubts. But a promise is a promise — so how could I get Pamela to guide a car?

The third week I couldn't see her every night because we had a few urgent repairs in. It was dreadful. The day seemed barren and pointless. Then, when I was testing this crazy old banger, I saw her wheeling a huge pram in the park.

THE next time I gave her a lesson I asked her about it and she said on fine days she always took a pramful and a couple of toddlers into the park. So all my test-drives ended up at the park gates and I'd sit and watch her pushing that pram.

And one day it came to me — just like that. There was this small, slim girl, shoving this heavy pram with one hand, the other tugging along a couple of toddlers, and she never put a foot — or rather a wheel — wrong! I couldn't have done it and I was twice her size.

That night as I waited outside her sister's flat I was almost jumping with excitement.

She smiled right at me and said, "I'm getting fond of that airfield."

"Not tonight," I said. "You're taking me to the wholesalers to pick up a new gearbox for a job we're doing."

Her eyes were enormous. "I'm taking you? You know I can't. You mean you'll drive."

I showed her my hand. I'd cut it through sheer negligence that morning and Ken had told me if I didn't keep my mind on the job it'd be my throat next.

"Can't manage it tonight, Pam. You'll be OK."

She stopped dead in her tracks. "I can't, Alan. Stop teasing me. You know I can't."

"You can't let me down, Pam. I've got to get that gearbox or Ken will chuck me out." I'd told her a thing or two over the fish and chips too. "You've had lots of practice ploughing round and round that field. It's only like pushing a pram and you do that easily enough."

She frowned. "You've been watching me."

"I certainly have. You're a wonderful pram pusher — one-handed, too. Sit in there and pretend it's a pram, Pam. I know you can do it, darling."

She went pink, very pink. Then she went and got into the driver's seat and started up. We'd only got about five yards when she flashed me a wonderful smile.

"Of course!" she carolled confidentally. "Why didn't I think of it before? It's easy, Alan!" She edged neatly up to a pedestrian crossing, paused and started over it with never a wobble.

I let Ken take her out after that and two weeks later I drove her into town for her test. She looked solemn and worried and her teeth gnawed away at her lower lip.

She hadn't been surprised when I stopped giving her lessons and she wasn't surprised to see me that morning. She knew more about me than I knew myself.

I nearly died waiting for her. I think I'd have throttled the examiner if he'd failed her. But, of course, he didn't. He knew a good driver when he saw one.

She came straight into my arms in the waiting-room. First, she cried into my neck and then she kissed me. I began to get that all-at-sea feeling again.

"Darling, I wanted to tell you, but you'd have said it didn't matter . . . and it did matter to me . . . can you understand?"

"No," I said truthfully.

> ### WANTED!
> A few weeks ago, I waited in a long bus queue. My bag was full of shopping and my feet ached.
>
> Along came the bus at last, and I was about to get on when the conductor announced, "Sorry, no room."
>
> But just then, a teenage boy got off the bus, saying, "You have my place, you are probably needed at home more than I am!"

"If I'd failed, Charles would have thrown me over and you would have picked me up. That would have been lovely, but I'd have been his — well his sort of *leavings*. I mean you took me on after the other places had thrown me out and I couldn't be thrown out *again*!

"You do understand, darling, don't you? I didn't want to prove anything for myself, but I didn't see why you should have to make do with a failure!"

I kissed her while everyone in the waiting-room watched. But I wasn't absolutely certain I understood. Sometimes I'm still unsure. But when you're deliriously happy you don't bother with a lot of questions, so it's not something that stops me sleeping.

One thing though. I never sent that bill to Clarkson for the lessons. Money can't buy what I've got, can it?

———— * **THE END** * ————

Complete Story
by
MALCOLM WILLIAMS

Thus far, he'd made a good job of bringing up his daughter on his own. But now, memories from the past began to shape the future . . .

Daddy's Girl

S TEVE HARPER'S anxieties over
the ice skating started just before
he moved house. He and his
daughter, Fiona, were rummaging up in
the loft, trying to classify things into
"usefuls" and "discards" when Fiona,
her eyes gleaming wonderingly, held up a
pair of old ice skates.

"I should put those back in the box,
Fiona," Steve told her abruptly. "They can
be dangerous!"

"But whose are they, Daddy?"

"Oh, they used to be your mother's, a long
time ago." Troubled, he watched his daughter
holding up the ice skates, a rapturous look on
her face.

And suddenly he felt anger rise within him —
against himself for not getting rid of those skates
years ago.

"Come on now, Fiona. We've a lot to do . . ."
Reluctantly, she put the skates back into the box, and
Steve hoped she'd just forget about them. But later, other
questions came:

"Was Mummy a good skater, Daddy?"

"Good?" Steve was tempted to lie, but he couldn't betray the
trust in his daughter's eyes.

"She was a brilliant skater, Fiona," he answered quietly. "She
was going to turn professional when —"

"When she was killed in the accident," Fiona completed the sentence.

"Ye-es." Steve nodded and made to move away. He anticipated and dreaded the next question.

"Can I keep the skates, please, Daddy?" his daughter said.

"What for, love?" he asked, trying to keep the tightness out of his voice, but failing.

"Well, they'd look nice hanging up in my bedroom. And —"

"And what?"

"They'd remind me of Mummy."

Steve turned to the window. Outside, dark clouds were scudding across the sky. He should have moved from this house straight after the accident, he told himself regretfully. He should have gone when Fiona was still a baby, and avoided this.

He could have, too. He could have changed his job, instead of waiting for promotion and transfer to another town.

Behind him, Fiona's voice was wistful.

"All I've got to remember Mummy by is her photograph, Daddy," she said softly.

Steve forced himself to smile, then turned around. "Of course you can keep the ice skates, darling," he said quickly. "If it will make you happy."

Fiona's face flushed with delight and she ran to put her arms round his neck. "Oh, thank you, Daddy!"

CRAYHAMPTON was a bustling, growing town and Steve welcomed the change. A senior accountant with his firm now, he had an office of his own, and enough money to make a proper home for Fiona.

Above all, he had a chance to finally erase the past, especially the memory of Laura and her ice skating.

It was twelve years ago now, but he'd never been able to forget what it had done to his life.

His wife had been driving home from an ice skating championship in a distant town when she and her skating partner had been killed in a pile-up on a foggy motorway. Fiona had been just a year old at the time.

In all the years since then, he'd never spoken of his wife's ice skating. And now he was more determined than ever not to remind himself of those days.

Yet Fate seemed to be working against him. For Fiona hung her mother's ice skates in her room, and seemed to look on them as her most precious possession.

And one evening, after she'd done her homework, she came downstairs and sat beside Steve on the couch.

"Have you got any photographs of Mummy actually skating, Daddy?" she asked softly, and Steve felt suddenly hollow.

Memories flooded over him. Memories of Laura — and the skating that had ruined their marriage . . .

Laura had been furious when she'd discovered she was pregnant. "I've got talent," she'd railed at him. "Star qualities, that's what Clive Stanway reckons. And he should know."

"Clive Stanway is an exhibitionist and a bachelor, Laura. He hasn't a home to consider. A child on the way . . ."

But nothing he'd been able to say had pacified her. She'd resented every moment of her pregnancy. Within three months of Fiona's birth, Laura had gone back to the ice rink — and Clive Stanway . . .

"Daddy . . .?"

Steve blinked, then nodded. "A photograph, Fiona?" he said. "Yes, I think I've got one tucked away somewhere . . ."

"I'll help you look for it, Daddy," Fiona said emphatically.

★　　　★　　　★　　　★

During the early weeks in their new home, Fiona continued to keep her mother's memory alive. And the photograph they'd found excited her as much as the ice skates hanging on her bedroom wall.

Steve cursed himself for keeping that photograph. It had been taken only a few months after their wedding, with Laura posing theatrically for the camera.

The photographer had known his job. Laura, in leotard and tights, her blonde hair coiled about her elegant head, looked stunning. On tiptoe, her ice skates making her look like a ballerina, her long shapely legs and artistic fingers had captured the essence of her gracefulness — and restlessness.

The full, generous smile was too generous in Steve's view, and the eyes . . .?" Yes, he still had to admit they were beautiful . . .

DARE YOU!

Near my home there runs a lovely river. In all the ten years that I have lived here, I have always had a longing to go paddling in it.

However, I could never find the courage to go down to the water. It would seem foolish, a middle-aged woman like me paddling.

Earlier this year, however, I had to spend some time in hospital. Lying in my hot bed, I made up my mind that as soon as I could I would have that paddle, never mind what people thought.

When I was fit enough, I walked to the river and did just that. It was really wonderful, standing there ankle deep in that cold, clear water. In future I shall do it any time it takes my fancy.

Foolish or not, it's worth it.

"She's very lovely, Daddy. Why didn't we have this photograph in the lounge before now?" Fiona's innocent words shook him and he took a moment to answer.

"I — I always preferred the wedding photographs, darling. The one taken of Mummy and Daddy together."

Together! The wedding photograph was a farce. It was only for his daughter's sake he'd kept it on display all these years. His marriage had been a mistake . . .

Continued overleaf

Continued from previous page

"Daddy . . .?" Fiona looked up to him, her eyes suddenly coy and appealing.

"Yes, love?"

"Daddy, do you think I could have skating lessons?"

Steve's insides knotted. But he knew there was no real argument against the request. He pointed out that she already played the piano, went horse riding at weekends. And she was still a bit young . . .

"How old was Mummy when she started skating then?"

"She was . . . as a matter of fact . . . she was only eight."

"But that's younger than me, Daddy!"

"Yes." He sighed, and nodded. "All right," he said. "I'll make some enquiries, Fiona."

AFTERWARDS he regretted his decision. He'd always prided himself on the way he'd reared Fiona almost single-handed.

She'd never been a demanding child, but he'd always done everything he could to ensure she was happy. An only child was a lonely child. An only parent was a lonely parent . . . He'd been sensitive to these facts, and had lived by them.

So although he regretted his decision, he didn't go back on his word.

Mrs Carstairs, his widowed, matronly secretary, was a remarkable woman. She more than anyone had helped him settle into his new

64

Those Country Capers!

Moving my family from the big city to life on a farm promised no end of excitement, says Margaret Finch. But that, as it turned out, was the understatement of the year!

EVERYONE knows that witches, wart-charmers, faith-healers and fairies - at - the - bottom - of - the-garden all abound in the West Country. So I shouldn't really have been surprised when we came to live in Devon to find that we too had our very own fairy — a mischievous sprite who kept a watchful eye on me and on the way I dressed, in particular!

Well, how else could I explain the catastrophes that befell me whenever I donned a dress or skirt?

It all started when my husband became redundant and we had to leave our comfortable house in a Birmingham suburb to start a new life on a small-holding in the country.

It took me no time at all to realise that barbed-wire fences and tight skirts just don't go together. Neither, for that matter, do high heels and muddy fields or

Continued overleaf

job at the office. She was confessor, counsellor and comrade as well as being a good secretary.

She sounded particularly interested when Steve mentioned that Fiona wanted to start ice skating.

"My niece might help you there, Mr Harper," she said. "You must have seen her. She works in the Admin Block, assistant to the personnel officer . . ."

"Ah yes . . ." Steve remembered Josie Franklin vaguely. A quiet young woman with short dark hair, neat as an acorn cap . . .

"Josie goes skating at the Southampton ice rink, Mr Harper," Mrs Carstairs explained. "She does it mostly for the exercise, I think. You know, sitting behind a typewriter all day . . .?"

She smiled. "Anyway, I'll mention it to her, Mr Harper."

Next morning, Josie Franklin came into Steve's office.

She wore a crisp white blouse and dark slim skirt; her fair hair was swept back at the front and sides, and her smile was engaging. "My aunt said I might be able to help you, Mr Harper," she said. "I'm going skating at the weekend. Would your daughter like to come, too?"

Steve had mixed feelings.

"I don't want to interfere with your plans, Miss Franklin," he began hesitantly. "I mean, won't you be going with friends . . .?"

"I always go alone." Her smile widened. "Actually, I'm a rotten skater. I like to lose myself in anonymous crowds . . ."

Continued overleaf

Continued from previous page
clean dresses and playful calves!

However, I learned quickly and by the time we had finished decorating our new home and patched up the fences and out-buildings I had almost forgotten there were such things as hairstyles and manicures. I was well and truly converted to living life in scruffy slacks and shirts.

Or I thought I was — until the day I caught sight of myself in the bedroom mirror! Whatever would my friends think of me, dressed like this? Most of them would be horrified that I'd let myself go! I had to take myself in hand.

I RUSHED through those early-morning chores and, hoping that I wouldn't be missed for a couple of hours, I jumped into a bath, washed and set my hair.

I sailed downstairs later, all aglow with confidence and clean-liness. But the illusion was im-mediately shattered by my husband who'd just come in.

"Ah," he said quickly. "Just in time! Two tons of hay have arrived. You'll have to help the driver un-load it."

All right, so he'd strained his back and couldn't do it himself. But at least he might have noticed I'd changed! Resignedly, I pulled off my clean dress, put on my trousers and manoeuvred myself to the top of the hay wagon to throw down the bales.

By the next day I was so stiff that I gratefully bared my sore limbs to the sunshine and relaxed in a deck-chair in the garden.

My sunbathing lasted for 10 blissful minutes and then pan-demonium broke loose!

"Mum, look out! Behind you!"

I opened my eyes wearily at the children's excited screams. What I saw made me break all speed records as I raced out of my chair.

The place was full of monsters! Three huge bullocks were demolish-ing the roses, while the others were eyeing my vegetable patch. Even more were coming at me through the ever-widening gap in the thorn hedge!

Grabbing the nearest weapon, I joined in the counter-attack against the invaders. Then, sadly retrieving my trousers, I spent the rest of the day repairing the damage!

In the weeks that followed, one minor disaster followed another. We put them all down to in-

---

Continued from previous page
"I don't want to put you out, Miss Franklin. My daughter's quite a handful. She could fall . . . hurt herself . . ."

Josie Franklin shook her head. "No, Mr Harper." She looked at him closely, and grinned. "Don't be a stick-in-the-mud," she said lightly. "Will your daughter be free this Saturday morning?"

Steve stared at her for a moment, then returned her smile. "Yes, Miss Franklin, she will."

By Saturday morning, Fiona was a bundle of nerves and excitement. She was dressed and ready to go, watching at the apartment window, as Steve was still shaving. With a half-shaved face, he paused and considered his reflection in the mirror. Were his eyes really too solemn, his jaw too stern, he wondered.

Laura had accused him often enough of being a killjoy. But then he'd never agreed with her idea of excitement.

experience until my daughter thoughtfully remarked:

"It's a funny thing, Mum, but these things always happen when you're wearing a skirt!"

It seemed incredible but it was true. I had to admit it as I remembered how I always had to go and change into trousers during an emergency and leave the kids to help my husband.

SPRING was on the way when I — or that mischievous sprite — caused the first "major" tragedy.

There was a touch of frost in the air when we returned from church on Easter Sunday. So, instead of changing into trousers, I kept my best suit on, determined that this was to be my day of rest. My family have never forgiven me.

By three o'clock that afternoon I was back in trousers and running to and fro with buckets of hot water for the vet — our pregnant cow had premature twins and naturally I alone was to blame!

That convinced me. No more dresses! And harmony reigned throughout the next few months as I slopped around in my old clothes, abandoning all pretence of being anything but a unisex farm-hand!

By the end of the summer, though, my husband felt in need of a break and accepted an invitation to stay with friends in Ireland. We all went to the airport to see him off and as it was a hot day I decided to risk it. After all, it would be his last sight of me for some time! So — I dressed up. No sooner had we got into the airport lounge when an announcement came over the loudspeaker. It was received in stony silence, until my young son turned to me.

"The plane is forty minutes late because of a technical fault," he repeated. "Now it's going to crash and it's all your fault — you're wearing a dress!"

But our mischievous sprite, for that's who I continued to blame, seemed to be losing interest. My husband returned safely, much refreshed, and at last I'd learned my lesson.

The last two or three years have been blessedly peaceful. Our sprite is probably too lethargic nowadays to rouse himself on the few odd occasions when I tempt him. Or maybe he just approves of the present trend in fashion — after all, one can at least feel feminine in a smartly-cut trouser suit! ∎

"You're nothing but an exhibitionist!" he'd shouted at her the night she'd gone off to that final skating championship. And he'd meant it. She hadn't seemed happy unless she was the centre of attraction, displaying her talent on the skating rink. And the more trophies she and Clive Stanway had won, the more ambitious she'd got.

Success, Steve thought, that was all that had mattered . . . He sighed. Now Fiona, so innocent, so trusting, was about to be unwittingly caught up in it all. And what made it worse was that Fiona was beginning to look like a cameo of her late mother.

"Miss Franklin's here, Daddy! Quickly!"

Hurriedly, Steve finished shaving. He was buttoning his shirt cuff as he came into the lounge. Fiona had already answered the door and Josie Franklin, in slacks and a sweater with an enormous collar, her

Continued overleaf

Continued from previous page
suede jacket open, was talking companionably.

"I'm not very keen on the Miss Franklin bit, Fiona," she was saying. "Makes me sound like an ageing spinster. I'm Josie."

She looked up. "Hello, Mr Harper."

Steve smiled.

"OK," Fiona agreed. "Will I be able to hire skates today, Josie?"

"Sure. Perhaps later your dad will buy you a pair of your own?"

Steve met Josie Franklin's eyes, and shrugged. "See how you get on first, Fiona." He smiled, keeping his fears to himself.

He watched the departing car. His heart felt big for his chest. He had a crazy notion that Fiona was about to slide away from him. He was glad of the bedroom which needed painting . . .

FOR three hours Steve kept painting, his mind on Fiona. Half of him was hoping she was enjoying herself, but the other half was willing her not to take readily to the ice. He felt she's be safe with Josie Franklin. He liked and trusted the girl already, and Fiona had taken to her instantly.

But Josie's enthusiasm bothered him. Would she encourage Fiona — bring her back dazzled by the prospect of becoming an ice skater?

Steve lit another cigarette. He realised he'd been virtually chain-smoking since his daughter's departure . . .

Fiona was radiant when she came home. She bounded indoors and threw her arms round Steve's neck.

"It was marvellous, Daddy. Absolutely marvellous! You should have been there!"

"I'm no ice skater," Steve said, lightly, controlling his tension. He raised his eyes to Josie Franklin.

"How did she make out, Miss Franklin?"

"You can't call her Miss Franklin!" Fiona protested heatedly. "That's too spinsterish!"

"OK." Steve shrugged. "Josie then."

"She certainly enjoyed herself, Mr —"

"Steve."

"All right, Steve," She smiled. "We watched everyone else for the first half hour, just to get the feel of things —"

"And there was a professional couple practising there," Fiona put in. "They were brilliant, weren't they, Josie!"

"Ye-es." Steve caught the uncertain glance between Josie and his daughter. More positively, she added:

"They were very good, Steve. An up and coming Olympic couple. Fiona was lucky to see them in action." She paused. "I, er, hope you don't mind, but I booked an hour's tuition for Fiona next Saturday morning."

"But —"

"I'll be skating properly then," Fiona rushed in. "I clomped around for a bit on the ice today, Daddy. Josie said I looked good though."

"All right, Fiona." Steve nodded, and glanced at Josie.

"She wants to run before she can walk, Steve. Or rather, spin before she can stand." She smiled at Fiona. "Well I'm glad you enjoyed it."

"It was great! Josie took me for a doughnut afterwards. Two doughnuts. And a cup of hot chocolate."

"That's the only reason I go ice skating." Josie grinned. "I'm too fond of things like doughnuts and hot chocolate."

Steve laughed. He felt a curious sense of relief, for in that moment he realised Josie wouldn't be the one to get Fiona seriously interested in skating.

"Josie's got no worries about her figure, has she, Daddy?" His daughter's voice piped up.

"Er, no . . ."

"And I'm going to practise hard on the ice until I'm as good as . . ."

Briefly, Fiona's glance switched to the photograph of Laura on the sideboard.

"Well, I'll leave you to it, Fiona." Josie said.

"You'll stay and have a coffee with us." Steve offered. "Some lunch perhaps?"

WHERE DID YOU GET THAT HAT?

During a recent cold spell I was out shopping wearing my warm angora hat with the jersey side flaps tied under my chin.

As I paused to look in a shop window an elderly gentleman sidled up to me and asked if I had ever been to Blackpool.

Thinking this was a funny question to ask, I decided I'd better humour him and replied that I had, many times.

"Do you know," he replied, "I thought you 'ad. Everybody comes back from there wearing funny 'ats."

Maybe I should have hit him with my shopping bag!

[Or dashed home to embroider "Kiss Me Quick" on the front.]

"Thanks. But I'm meeting my aunt in ten minutes. She wants me to help her choose a new coat —" She looked at her watch. "Gracious! I must fly!"

For the remainder of the weekend, Fiona was full of ice skating — and Josie Franklin.

"Let's give the subject a rest," Steve pleaded on Sunday night as Fiona was getting into bed. "You've got school tomorrow, a week of work!"

Fiona pulled a face. She asked Steve to read her a favourite poem, and as he read, she lay, hands linked behind her head, staring at the ice skates on the opposite wall. Before the light went out, she gave Steve a hug.

"Thanks, Daddy, for making me happy. Will I be able to have new skates for next week?"

Continued on page 72

My Little Orphans Of The Storm

Sick and injured birds have descended on me over the years, says Mrs P. B. And there's nothing so wonderful — or so sad — as when those little creatures are able to fly away again . . .

I'VE always been interested in birds — one of my earliest memories is of watching the local sparrows going about their business. Even then, as a child, I thought how beautiful they were.

Over the years my interest grew, from just watching birds, feeding them, to helping injured, sick or orphaned fledglings. There was no-one to teach me about "bird doctoring." I learned the hard way and shed many bitter tears over my failures.

Now, because I have a good deal of practical experience, I can usually assess my patients chances.

Birds of passage, I call these unfortunate creatures. Their needs are modest: food, water, warmth, shelter and security.

In as little as 24 hours some can be released, and nothing gives me greater happiness than that moment when I can set them free.

Sometimes that moment may be long delayed but it is worth waiting for — always.

Often I am asked how I feel when the time comes for them to fly away. Naturally, I feel concern for them; how will they cope with freedom and the many problems it can bring? And, of course, I know that I am going to miss them quite horribly.

But the moment of release is a culmination of all I have worked for. Flight is their birth-right, liberty their heritage. It is the greatest happiness to me to think that in some small way I have been able to help them.

One example is Toby.

Our first acquaintance was when he had his head in the mouth of next-door's cat! Certainly not the most promising beginning, and when I rescued the tiny, woeful scrap there seemed small hope of his surviving.

personality pets *personality pets*

personality pets personality pets

A miniature sparrow, he was the runt discarded by his parents because he would never amount to much. His condition was poor and he was suffering from shock but he rallied well. A bright, intelligent bird, he quickly learned to feed himself.

However, his appearance deteriorated rather than improved. Added to that, he developed toe trouble and lost several joints before I was able to arrest the condition. He seemed quite unruffled, but I was worried to death!

If he'd had a gentle and affectionate nature, this would have made up for his downright ugliness. But for his size, Toby was the most ferocious and aggressive sparrow I have ever known with a truly excruciating peck.

Now, however, Toby has moulted into adult plumage. Now there are no shabby feathers, but a gleaming livery of chestnut and buff, the smart black bib of the cock sparrow and beautiful flashes of purest white in wings and tail.

When I eventually release him, some lucky hen will be very impressed with a magnificent Prince Charming. In fact, I have an idea whom she may be; more about her later . . .

CASS, short for Hopalong Cassidy, because he is permanently lame in one leg, is my starling. When I first saw him I again had doubts about his survival.

Only a few days earlier, a young thrush had been brought to me with similar injuries. I had been unable to save the thrush and had vowed to put to sleep immediately any bird maimed in the same way. But only one of Cass's legs was out of commission. Surely that meant a 50-50 chance?

How glad I am I took the risk.

Cass is an extrovert, Mr Personality-Plus — a born entertainer. He soon came to terms with his bad leg, developing great strength in the other.

In his roomy cage, life presents no problems. The best of food and attention have changed him from a modestly-clad fledgling to a resplendent fellow in irridescent feathers that

Continued overleaf

Continued from previous page
gleam with gold and green and purple, each one tipped with a white spot.

However, it worries me that I may never be able to let him go. Although now a reasonable flier, that lame leg is a big handicap.

An ardent sunbather, Cass should never have a personal freshness problem! The sight of his bath bowl produces excitement that reaches near hysteria. No testing the temperature of the water, plunk — straight in.

If I'm holding the bowl at the time I get splattered from head to foot as he bobs in and out of the water. Then, if he gets half a chance, Cass dashes up my arm and cuddles into my neck, clearly regarding me as a human feather-drier.

THE Tweedles arrived within a couple of days of each other. Dee came first, another small sparrow just needing a few days' grace to gather strength and experience. I almost trod on Dum the following day, a beautiful greenfinch cock.

People who know nothing about birds fondly imagine that all you have to do is toss them some scraps of bread, give them water and that is the end of your worries. Alas, such is not the case. The needs of each individual are different and until the bird knows how to eat alone, it is totally dependent on its foster-mother for survival. Take the Tweedles, for example.

Young mums often complain about disturbed nights with new babies and the fact that they have to be fed at four-hourly intervals. But at least their infants don't suddenly vanish under the bed!

Four o'clock in the morning is no time for playing hide-and-seek, and since little birds need feeding at far more frequent intervals than babies, I was literally bog-eyed until the Tweedles learnt to help themselves.

Their stay was brief. Within 10 days they were fully mobile, self-sufficient, and after a number of trials I reckoned they had both qualified for their certificate of airworthiness.

Just before "Liberation Day," when I was congratulating myself on the blissful prospect of well-earned relaxation ahead, Buffnut was brought to me.

Buffnut, another sparrow, is again a slow developer. There's nothing the matter with her except that she won't

Continued from page 69
"Only if you concentrate on your school work during the week," he teased.

Then, heavy-hearted, he went into the quiet, empty lounge . . .

THE following week was the start of the firm's annual stocktaking, and Steve scarcely looked up from the work on his desk. Then during Friday lunchtime, Josie Franklin sat down next to him in the canteen.

I thought I'd better check if it's still OK to take Fiona to the ice rink tomorrow, Steve." Her dark hair shone under the lights, and she looked quite lovely.

Steve gave her a rueful grin.

"Fiona's looking forward to it. Tell me, though, what did you mean when you said she wanted to run before she could walk?"

fly properly until she has moulted. Very tame at first, she was soon feeding herself. Shortly after the Tweedles had flown off gleefully, I took little Buffnut out to the huge cage where Toby reigned in solitary state.

At first I was afraid that he might bully her, but at this time he was even tinier than she, and the young madam made no bones about the fact that she was boss-bird.

Buffnut's early tameness soon wore off and she became excessibly timid. It's always a good thing when a bird is wary of prospective danger, but she had hysterics every day when I cleaned the cage.

In her panic, she would fly to the front of the cage and try to thrust her way through the bars. Several times she cut her face badly and I was at my wits' end to find a solution.

Then suddenly I had a bright idea. I went to the nearest haberdasher's and bought some cheap net and a packet of drawing pins. The net "curtains" on the inside of the sparrow's cage looked anything but professional, but they have certainly served their purpose. Now when the silly little thing gets in a flap, they prevent her doing herself any harm.

Visitors seeing their residence for the first time give me some very odd looks. Until I have had the chance to explain, I can almost see them wondering whether I've founded an enclosed order or whether the birds are being kept in some sort of purdah!

A while back I was talking about Toby and his possible future spouse. Well, maybe at the moment Buffnut doesn't look much of a pin-up from a bird's eye view but soon she will be going through her own transformation scene. So when I free Toby, Buffnut will go with him.

Now I don't normally go in for matchmaking, but secretly I'm hoping that those net curtains are really a premature bridal veil! ∎

"Just that she's dead keen to skate," Josie explained. "I understand her mother was an expert."

"Ye-es," Steve considered his dessert, then pushed it aside.

"And she's determined to impress her dad, of course," Josie added with a smile.

Steve nodded. "How, er, how do you think Fiona will shape up as a skater, Josie?"

"Who knows? But if her ability matches her enthusiasm . . ." She stood up. "Well, must fly, Steve. Stocktaking!" She pulled a face. "See you tomorrow."

Steve watched her go out through the swing doors. Her words echoed in his mind: *If her ability matches her enthusiasm . . .*

Fiona, he thought, would be set on the same glittering path her mother had taken . . .

Continued overleaf

Continued from previous page

FIVE weeks later, Fiona declared: "There's going to be a skating display at the rink. And I've been chosen to skate, Daddy."

Steve received the news tensely.

"Well done, darling," he said quietly. "You must be getting on very well."

"It's the skates you bought me, Daddy." Fiona kissed him happily. "They'd make anybody do well."

Steve smiled apprehensively. Fiona's Saturday ritual seemed to have been going on for ages.

Was it only such a short time ago, he pondered, that his daughter had accidentally found Laura's old skates? He tried to shake off the mood but it was impossible. Over the weeks a feeling of helplessness had come over him, and it weighed heavily. Even Josie had noticed it, and had told him smilingly to cheer up. But he'd been brusque and offhand, and when she'd left with Fiona for the rink, he'd seen the unhappiness in her eyes.

Since then, she hadn't exactly avoided him, but she no longer called down to chat over lunch, and she seemed strangely quiet.

Steve sighed. Despite his worries, he knew he had no right to be a — a killjoy . . .

IS your niece all right, Mrs Carstairs?" he asked his secretary next morning in the office. "She doesn't have much to say nowadays."

"Josie?" Mrs Carstairs looked thoughtfully across the carriage of her typewriter. "She's got a lot on her mind just now, Mr Haprer. But she's really wrapped up in your little girl. She used to be all dances and ten-pin bowling. Never a night at home . . .?"

At dinner, Steve made a point of seeing Josie in the canteen.

"What kind of display is it at the rink, then?" he asked lightly, as they sat down together.

THAT'S NO GHOST!

During one of our trips into the Derbyshire countryside last summer, we were walking up a long lane when we became aware of the wailing of bagpipes.

Hardly able to believe our ears, we walked closer and closer to the sound, imagining all sorts of things.

We were almost up to it, when suddenly it stopped. Holding our breath, we rounded the corner.

There he was! Not a phantom piper, but a perfectly ordinary chap, putting the bagpipes away in the boot of his car. He then drove off without a word.

We were left staring, assuming he had been driven to practising in the countryside to keep away from irate neighbours!

[Now that's what we call consideration.]

"Well, it's a family get-together really. The children are split into age groups, each doing a spot. You know, a big show for doting parents . . ."

Steve dropped his eyes.

"I'm sorry," Josie said. "I didn't mean it to sound that way."

For the first time since he'd known her she seemed embarrassed.

"Is there any chance of Fiona doubling up on her lessons between now and the display!" she asked after a moment.

"Why is that?"

"Well, she's only a novice, Steve, and everyone else has far more experience. Fiona's really keen to do well at this display."

"Following in Mother's footsteps —" Steve bit back the rest of the words, annoyed with himself.

Josie gave him a puzzled look, then said: "I could take her to Southampton mid-week. It's no trouble."

"But you've already done so much . . ."

"Please?"

Steve knew he couldn't refuse. It would help make up for his offhandedness and show he'd never meant to be deliberately unkind. She really was a very lovely girl.

"All right," he said, quietly. "With the proviso that you have dinner with me one evening soon. Please?"

She smiled for the first time.

"All right," she replied softly. "I'd like that, Steve."

BRIEF ENCOUNTER

A few years ago, when my brother lived in London, we didn't see each other for several months.

One day in the Underground he thought he saw me.

He rushed up to a girl, put his arms round her and gave her a big hug, with a "Hello, love! What are you doing here?"

A shocked-looking stranger turned round to face him.

"S — sorry, I thought you were my sister!" he said.

Strangely enough, that girl is related to us now. She is his wife and my sister-in-law!

A few evenings later, Steve caught Fiona in an unguarded moment. She was in the lounge with her back to him as he came in from running her bath, so she didn't hear him. She was staring at the photograph of her mother, and her stillness made her look as if she was in a trance.

A cold shiver passed down Steve's spine. He cleared his throat and Fiona started guiltily.

"A penny for them, Fiona?"

"Oh, I was just thinking, Daddy . . ."

It was obvious she wasn't going to tell him what she was thinking.

"Your bath's ready," he said. *Continued on page 79*

A Prayer

IN Jersey City, on the East Coast of America, one cold day in January 1950, my mother's doorbell rang. She opened it and found an American Air Force officer and a priest outside.

They had come to tell her that my husband and I were missing, presumed dead.

The priest told my mother the details — the small plane piloted by my husband, Donald, and with me aboard, had gone down somewhere in the wilderness of Alaska. An intensive search had failed to find us.

"There is little or no hope now of finding your daughter and her husband alive," he finished.

At that time, Donald and I had in fact been missing for 10 days.

It all started when we had received an emergency radio message from a small settlement about 250 miles to the north-east of our home in Fairbanks, Alaska. A doctor had to perform an emergency operation and needed drugs and the assistance of a qualified nurse.

However, the only nurse serving the North was ill. I volunteered to accompany my husband as I had trained as a nurse. Our children were left with our neighbours and as snow threatened from a leaden sky we took off.

We ran into a severe blizzard and Donald had to make a forced landing. Neither of us was hurt but the plane was wrecked in the deep snow

and the radio was out of commission

We knew, as we huddled in the shelter of the fuselage, that there wa little hope for us unless by some miracle someone spotted us from the air.

We had a bottle of brandy and some food but with the temperature far below freezing point, Donald and realised that our chances of surviva were slight.

But there was one faint hope — m mother. You see, she had a strange almost frightening gift.

She could see things as they happened by concentrating her mind o someone. I had known about this gi ever since I was a little girl and

76

Away From Death

Mother had often told me, "Clare, if ever you are in danger, concentrate on me and try to send me a message.

"If you think hard enough and concentrate hard enough you may be quite certain that I will receive your message."

Now, as we faced death, I tried to concentrate on my mother, but not very successfully.

This was probably because I don't suppose I really believed strongly enough. However, on that tenth afternoon, when the blizzard abated a little, I walked outside and stood a

few paces from the wreckage of the plane. I looked west towards a snow-capped mountain and concentrated on it.

It was about seven miles from us but as the sky cleared a little it became quite clear. It had a curious shape, like a polar bear, but the nearer peak looked like an eagle in flight.

It was the kind of mountain that, although only a little over three thousand feet high, stood out in the wilderness like a beacon because of its strange shape.

I put everything out of my mind; thoughts about the wilderness, my children, and of death as I fixed my eyes on that mountain and concentrated on my mother.

My husband didn't come near me but left me alone as I stood there, forcing my mind to concentrate.

Then I spoke aloud. "Mother, we are alive, we are well, but we cannot survive long," I said. "Here is a land-mark — if the search pilot can find this mountain they will find us."

Continued overleaf

The Authorities held out little hope for my husband and I — lost in Alaska's frozen wilderness. But they reckoned without the remarkable gift of my mother. She could "see" where I was . . .

77

Continued from previous page

Keeping my gaze fixed on the mountain, I closed my eyes. I remember a solitary teardrop rolling unheeded down my cheek. I stood there for perhaps another 10 minutes, then I turned and got back into the fuselage of the plane and had a small drink of brandy.

I will never know why but as I sat down, I said to my husband, "Don, have the petrol can ready. I am quite certain that rescue will come tomorrow."

He didn't reply to that but merely looked at me. Eventually, he said, "Your mother?"

I nodded. He knew about Mother's strange gift from incidents in the past.

IN Jersey City — I am of course telling you what I learned later — Mother was having a late tea when she "saw" my husband and me huddled by the plane.

Mum "saw" a vast snow-covered landscape and in the distance, a peculiar-shaped mountain. She heard me call to her and ask her to help. She took up a pad and pencil and as she "saw" the mountain she began to sketch it and to sketch the whole terrain to show where the wreckage of the plane was to be found.

Then the vision faded out but she had the sketch. She donned her coat and telephoned the only people she could think of who might be able to help quickly — the FBI. They told her to go to their local office and she took a taxi there.

The FBI called up the USAF station at Fairbanks, Alaska, and spoke to a senior officer. When the officer replaced the receiver, he told my mother, "We have orders to get this sketch flown to Fairbanks as quickly as possible."

They were as good as their word. A fighter plane was called in, the sketch handed over and within hours of my mother leaving the FBI office, the jet was winging its way through the night skies to distant Alaska.

There, officers studied my mother's map. Several knew of the mountain but they could not figure how we could have got to there. It was considerably off course.

Nevertheless, at first light five Air Force planes took off and headed for the mountain.

We heard the distant whine of the jets and though we could not see them in the wintry sky, Donald poured petrol over the pile of wreckage he had built and ignited it.

A flame and a pall of smoke rose into the sky and within two or three minutes a jet fighter whined overhead and swooped low. Then it veered round and dropped packages to us, containing a stout tent, food, drink, even a portable gas heater.

"It is too far for a helicopter to land," Donald said, when they'd gone. "They'll have to send in a light plane, so I'm going to lay out a landing path for him."

With fuel from the plane's petrol tank, my husband prepared flares and laid them out on a flat strip of snow-covered land. Then we waited, comfortable now, knowing that we would live.

Just after dawn the next day the small plane came overhead. Donald rushed out, laid the flares and lit the landing path. We watched as the plane touched down on its skis then we ran to greet the pilot. We clambered aboard and were whisked off to safety.

I telephoned my mother as soon as we reached Fairbanks.

"I knew you would be safe, Clare," she told me. "I got your message." ■

Continued from page 75

After her bath, Fiona went upstairs to bed. Steve sat by the fire, book on his lap, unable to concentrate on reading.

In a way he knew it was simply that he regretted that Fiona had to grow up. If only she didn't look so much like her mother, he thought. All he wanted was for her to be happy. But right then he would have given anything to have heard her say:

"I've tried skating, Daddy, and I don't like it."

Instead, she seemed utterly devoted to her Saturday morning trips to the ice rink with Josie. And now, with the extra mid-week lessons, conversation centred around nothing else but the coming display . . .

Steve stood up abruptly, his book fluttering to the floor. Catching sight of Laura's photograph on the sideboard, he felt numb. Her

"A Story Of Courage . . ."

IT'S a well-used phrase, that, isn't it?

But, as with all oft-used phrases, the meaning becomes blurred.

Over the past few weeks I have had personal experience of a story of courage that, for me, threw the meaning into needle-sharp focus.

No, it didn't involve a dramatic rescue or an act of heroism on some foreign battlefield. It concerned a very dear friend of mine — a housewife going about the business of a perfectly ordinary life.

A small physical discomfort had resulted in her going into hospital for a minor operation.

She came round from the anaesthetic to discover that she had undergone a far-from-minor operation and that the surgeon had discovered she had been really quite ill.

She was told that her post-operative treatment would take months.

I went to see her in hospital soon afterwards. As I went into the small side ward I was astonished to be greeted by a bright-eyed — yes, radiant — young woman. She was sitting up in bed, wearing an attractive bed jacket and chatting animatedly to her husband and two children.

We had a few minutes alone, and I remarked on how well she looked.

She leaned over and smiled wryly. "I nearly gave up, you know," she told me quietly. "But, suddenly, I remembered how much I had — how many people cared about me."

She flashed another wide smile. "After that, it was easy."

That was nearly two months ago. She hasn't fooled me. She's on the mend now, but it certainly has not been easy.

But anyone who looked at her anxiously in that time received in return that flashing, all-concealing smile.

Now that's courage!

smile taunted him. Slowly, he went upstairs to Fiona's bedroom.

She was fast asleep, one hand characteristically thrown out, her hair spilling over the pillow. She was so young and vulnerable, he thought. On the opposite wall, the moonlight shafted directly on to the ice skates . . .

STEVE was nervous about taking Josie out to dinner. He'd dressed carefully, conscious that during the past few years he'd rarely been in another woman's company, unless it had been in a crowd.

The babysitter arrived on time and he went into Fiona's bedroom to kiss her goodnight.

"You look very handsome, Daddy. You should go out more often."

"Thanks."

At the door he paused, reluctant to leave her.

"You're looking forward to seeing me skate at the display, aren't you, Daddy?"

"You bet I am, love," he lied.

"I hope you'll have a nice surprise," Fiona said. "It'll be the first time you've watched me."

Then in a strained sort of voice she added: "Mummy would have wanted me to be a good skater, wouldn't she?"

"Sure she would." Steve nodded reassuringly. "Sweet dreams, darling . . ."

He arrived early at Josie's flat, but she was ready. In the hallway he helped her slip a coat over her long dress, and for a moment his hands rested on her shoulder. She turned to him, her face serious.

"Steve is everything all right?" she asked quietly. "You seem worried . . ."

The concern in her eyes made him feel suddenly ashamed.

"Everything's fine, Josie," he said. "Just fine."

They had a quiet Italian meal at a small candlelit restaurant. But despite the cosy atmosphere and Josie's presence, Steve gradually became more and more subdued.

"Things hectic at work, Steve?"

"Not especially. Stocktaking is over now."

"Fiona's devoted to you, isn't she?" Josie said softly, after a moment. "You must be very proud of her."

"Uh-huh."

"She doesn't remember her mother, I understand."

"No." Steve studied his wine glass. "Josie, would you say that Fiona has natural skating ability?"

"You've asked me that before, Steve. Why? Does it worry you?"

"Oh, no reason . . ."

Her grey eyes were searching. "Well, let's say that Fiona's throwing everything she's got into the ice skating, Steve. She's really

Continued on page 86

A Taste Of The
Orient

Succulent recipes from China, Japan and Thailand specially for you!

China

China

Chinese food is colourful and very flavoursome. No special equipment is needed, although it is fun to use a wok rather than a conventional frying-pan. Chinese cooks cut their ingredients into very small pieces, often shredding or slicing into very thin slivers so that the food cooks very quickly indeed.

TAIPAN SOUP

4 oz. lamb's liver.
1 small onion.
1 piece stem ginger, peeled or
½ teaspoonful dried.
1 tablespoonful cooking oil.
10 oz.-can Campbell's Cream of Tomato soup.
1 tablespoonful soy sauce.
2 spring onions.

Slice the liver into wafer-thin pieces. Very finely chop the onion and the piece of stem ginger.

Heat the oil in a frying-pan or wok and stir fry for two minutes.

Put the tomato soup, soy sauce and ½ pint water into a saucepan and add the liver, onion and ginger. Bring to the boil, stirring continuously, then lower the heat and simmer for 5 minutes.

Serve with thinly-sliced spring onion.
Serves 4.

Pagoda outside Nanking

CHICKEN WITH LEMON SAUCE

4 chicken breasts, skinned.
2 egg yolks.
2 teaspoonfuls dry sherry.
2 teaspoonfuls soy sauce.
2 oz. cornflour.

For The Sauce:

Zest and juice of 1 small lemon.
1 level teaspoonful sugar.
10 oz.-can Campbell's Cream of Chicken soup.
Slices of lemon to garnish.

Lay the chicken breasts in a shallow dish.

Mix the egg yolks, dry sherry and soy sauce together. Add 1 level dessertspoonful of the cornflour and blend together. Pour over the chicken and chill for about 30 minutes.

Remove from the marinade and coat with the remaining cornflour. Fry until golden brown and thoroughly cooked, drain and cut chicken into diagonal strips. Arrange on a hot serving plate.

Blend the sauce ingredients together and bring to the boil, stirring occasionally.

Garnish the chicken with slices of lemon and serve the sauce separately.
Serves 4.

Japan

Japanese food is always light to eat and attractive to the eye with ingredients fresh and of the highest quality. Preparation should be thorough and cooking fast, using a minimum of fat for a healthy diet.

CHICKEN AND VEGETABLES IN MUSHROOM SAUCE

8 small mushrooms.
8 oz. cooked chicken, finely shredded.
2 oz. carrot, cut into matchstick-size pieces and blanched.
10 oz.-can Campbell's Cream of Mushroom soup.
½ pint milk.
4 eggs.
Salt and pepper.

Divide the mushrooms, chicken and carrots into four ½-pint soup bowls.

Whisk the soup, milk and eggs together. Season with salt and pepper and pour into the bowls.

Stand the bowls in a roasting tin and pour in boiling water to come halfway up the bowls. Cook at 350 deg. F., 180 deg. C., Gas Mark 4, for 40-50 minutes or until just set in the middle.

Serve as a starter or light lunch dish.

Serves 4.

A geisha is a member of a professional class of women in Japan whose occupation is to entertain men, particularly at businessmen's parties in public restaurants.

The word geisha literally means art person," and many of the women sing, dance, or play musical instruments, though the majority are adept only in the art of conversation.

FOIL-BAKED SALMON AND VEGETABLES

½ oz. butter.
4 salmon or cod steaks.
1 small carrot, thinly sliced.
½ small green pepper, thinly sliced.
4 spring onions, sliced lengthways.
4 tablespoonfuls Campbell's Cream of Mushroom soup blended with four tablespoonfuls water.
Lemon to garnish.

Lightly rub the dull side of four 10 in.-square pieces of foil with butter.

Lay the salmon steaks in the centre of the foil and cover with the vegetables.

Spoon two level tablespoonfuls of the soup on to each piece and seal the foil to make a tight parcel.

Place on a baking sheet and cook for 15 minutes at 375 deg. F., 190 deg. C., Gas Mark 5.

Serve with slices of lemon.

Serves 4.

GEISHA GIRLS

83

Thailand

Trade links with India, China and Indonesia have influenced the cuisine of Thailand. Thai cooking is spicy and often very hot. The "fire" is put into these dishes with chilli peppers which are often just too much for Western palates to cope with.

CURRIED CHICKEN

½ oz. butter.
1 tablespoonful vegetable oil.
8 chicken thigh pieces, skinned.
1 onion, chopped.
1 clove garlic, crushed.
2 level tablespoonfuls curry powder.
10 oz.-can Campbell's Consommé.
3 oz. desiccated coconut, liquidised with ¼ pint boiling water.
1 level tablespoonful cornflour, mixed with a little of the consommé.

Heat the butter and oil in a large saucepan and brown the chicken all over. Remove with a draining spoon and set aside.

Cook the onion and garlic until soft but not brown. Stir in the curry powder, consommé, coconut and cornflour.

Add the chicken. Cover and simmer for 45 minutes until tender.

Arrange the chicken on a hot serving dish and pour a little of the curry sauce over. Serve the rest separately. Serve with rice.
Serves 4.

LEMON FISH

10 oz.-can Campbell's Cream of Celery soup.
1 lb. monkfish tail or cod, cut into bite-sized pieces.
Zest and juice of 1 large lemon.
2 fresh chilli peppers, seeded and very thinly sliced OR 1 level teaspoonful chilli pepper.
3 spring onions, trimmed and finely sliced.

Pour the soup into a saucepan and stir in 8 fluid oz. water.

Stir in the fish, lemon zest, juice and the chilli. Simmer for 10 minutes.

Pour into a large serving bowl and sprinkle the sliced spring onion on top.

Japan

Thailand

Continued from page 80
intent on proving something. You'll see that at the display next week."

Steve sighed. That's what he'd feared. Fiona was desperately trying to follow in Laura's footsteps. Attempting to copy the talents of the mother she'd never known . . .

Josie was still watching him curiously.

"Fiona's a credit to you, Steve. You've worked wonders rearing a bright, spirited girl like that. It seems wrong that you should be so anxious."

"Sorry, Josie. I'm dull company. How about some brandy?"

"Why not," She smiled, but the smile didn't reach her eyes.

D URING the following week, Steve worried a lot about the coming skating display. He couldn't lose the feeling of inevitability now. There was nothing he could do to prevent his daughter becoming obsessed with the glamour of ice skating, and that, it seemed, was exactly what she seemed to be.

Every night now she went to the rink to practise, coming home red-faced, tired, but triumphant, her ice skates slung across one shoulder.

Steve had never known her to be so determined to excel at anything. And the night before the display she couldn't sleep for excitement.

Steve sat up half the night himself, chain-smoking, trying desperately to be reasonable. But apprehension and resentment were like lead in his stomach.

By morning, however, he managed to welcome Josie with a smile. He felt strangely warmed by her presence.

He drove to the ice rink slowly, his eyes on the traffic, yet conscious of Fiona's excited skating talk coming from the back.

It was Sunday afternoon and the ice rink was packed with spectators.

"Well, Daddy, this is it." Fiona smiled nervously, and squeezed his hand.

"Good luck," he told her in a strange voice.

Then Josie led her over to the other children, standing in a circle round the organisers.

Steve watched in a kind of daze, then Josie was back at his side, leading him to a seat at the rink.

They didn't have long to wait. Music blared across the ice rink. Then the display sequence was announced over the public address system.

It was novices first. Steve was hardly aware of Josie's shoulder against his as Fiona came on to the ice. Although she resembled her late mother, Steve was surprised at how gangly she looked on skates, like a newly-born foal trying to find its legs.

"Miss Fiona Harper, from Crayhampton," the loudspeaker music eased across the ice, something light and rhythmic and simple. And with a brave smile, Fiona raised her arms and began to skate.

She didn't move far away from the safety barrier but skated in awkward little sequences, sometimes missing the beat of the music, sometimes frowning as she sought to adjust a faulty movement.

Sympathetic sighs from on-lookers reminded Steve that he wasn't dreaming. That was his daughter out there, doing her best, giving it all she'd got — but struggling!

Despite Fiona's attractive costume, her carefully-bobbed hair and the determination puckering her face, the most untrained observer could see that she wasn't a born ice skater. Even when the music ended and she dropped an inexpert curtsy, producing thunderous applause of encouragement, Steve knew that his daughter was never going to follow in her mother's footsteps.

JUST PICTURE IT!

Do you remember the good old days before central heating when we could sit by the fire seeing pictures in the glowing coals? Well, I've found a substitute.

We've recently had the bathroom decorated with the marbled tiles. Each is different, and in the markings so far I've found a bald man with a large droopy nose, a perky dog, a happy, giant caterpillar and "Jaws."

It has one advantage over the fire, too — the pictures don't vanish and you can enlarge your collection.

I'm now thinking of having an armchair installed for more comfortable viewing!

His hands were stinging from applauding so much. His eyes were blurred as he watched Fiona move off the ice and make way for the next skater.

Josie's voice was soft against his ear.

"She was so determined to please you, Steve."

"I know, Josie. Now I know . . ."

Steve felt dazed from the sudden realisation that Fiona had wanted to skate like her mother, only because she'd thought it would please and make him happy . . .

"I . . . didn't like to say anything to you before, Steve," Josie said quietly. "In case you expected her to be brilliant, too."

Steve looked at her and smiled. She was so apprehensive, so very lovely, so . . .

He seized both her hands in his. "Josie, I think you're wonderful!" he shouted. "Come on!"

He drew her to her feet, oblivious to everyone else around them. They hurried out to the entrance, where Fiona was sitting holding her skates.

Her eyes lip up as she saw Steve.

"Well, Daddy. How . . . how was I?"

"How were you?" He hugged his daughter, lifting her high in the air. "You were marvellous. That's what you were, darling. Ruddy marvellous!"

———— * **THE END** * ————

IT WAS THAT KIND OF A DAY, WHEN A WIFE IS ABLE TO LOOK AT HER MARRIAGE AND ASK HERSELF...

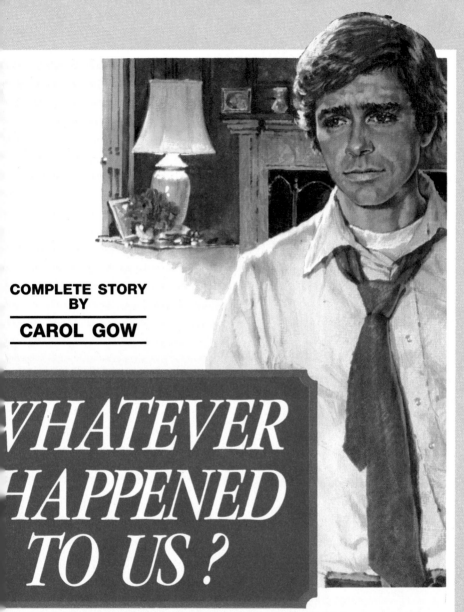

**COMPLETE STORY
BY**

CAROL GOW

WHATEVER HAPPENED TO US ?

AT that moment, the paper dress pattern she'd been searching
for went from Gillian Webster's head completely. Her hand
fell with delight on the tattered old buff folder.

She sat down on the bare attic floor, smiling at her discovery.
Eagerly, she sifted through its contents. A concert programme, a
menu, postcards from Venice, exam certificates . . . and a slim,
leather-bound diary.

She flicked through the pages. Most of them were empty, apart from scrawled times, meeting places, a birthday reminder. She smiled. *Ken 7.30.*

Of course, it was the year she'd met Ken, her husband. She looked through the other pages with interest. If only she'd kept a proper diary, something to look back on . . .

But the book was filled with the briefest of notes. A Christmas present, probably, that she'd used for the first couple of months of the year, then forgotten about.

She stopped suddenly at a page covered with a close, firm scrawl that filled the page and wound almost illegibly up and round the margins of the paper.

Her forehead wrinkled as she tried to make out the words. There were a couple at the beginning which had faded to obscurity, but she made out the rest . . .

— fortune tonight. Wined, dined and danced — great! Flowers, too, for my birthday. Was almost sick with excitement. Felt sure Ken going to propose but no, not yet. I was nervous in case he did. He was edgy, too. Soon, I think, I hope! Marvellous, marvellous man. Mrs Ken Webster!

Everyone in bed, no-one to talk to. Can't sleep — so happy, want to do all the corny things. Sing in rain, dance in street . . . can't wait till tomorrow —

She flicked carefully over the rest of the pages, but she hadn't written again. Then, on December 11, there it was. *St Margarets 1.30.*

Her wedding day.

She closed the diary slowly and wedged it back among the documents in the folder and replaced it in the cupboard.

Then, her mind still dwelling on the diary, she went downstairs into the kitchen. She stacked the tea dishes in the basin and ran hot water over them.

Just a few words on one page, yet somehow the hurried scrawl had made that time come back to her so vividly she could almost taste it, smell it.

The headlines of that first summer; rushing from the college gates, across the park to where Ken would be waiting for her . . .

Caught up for a moment in the memory, she glanced at her face, mirrored against the dark glass of the window.

Slowly, she raised her hand, almost certain that she would feel the weight of her hair, flowing past her shoulders to her waist . . .

B UT it was a different Gillian who stared back, wide eyed, at her, the mouth suddenly sad. Her hair, frothy and bubbly, clung in tendrils around her face. She pressed her forehead against the cool of the window, and an unreasonable feeling of slow terror enveloped her, swallowing her up.

What happened to us? she mouthed soundlessly. Ken and Gill scurrying through the streets to catch a film, sitting for hours over a single cup of coffee . . . So much talking, so much laughing to

CLARK GABLE

★★★★★★★★★★★★★★★★★★

'When Howard Hughes was called to watch Clark Gable auditioning for a film rôle he dismissed him with the words, "His ears make him look like a taxi-cab with both doors open."

Gable was painfully aware of this drawback, and for a long time allowed the make-up artists to tape his ears back.

Then one day he was filming a scene with Greta Garbo when the tape snapped and an ear flapped loose. No-one noticed — and that was the end of the tape.

———————— • ————————

When Clark Gable took off his shirt in *It Happened One Night*, and revealed that he wasn't wearing a vest, sales of undershirts plummeted almost overnight. '

★★★★★ ★★★★★★★★★★★★★★★★★★★★★★★★

do . . . Ken, his jacket slung across one shoulder, talking earnestly, endlessly, about their plans for the future . . .

Was it so long ago? Too long ago? Gillian dried the dishes and put them away. She glanced at her watch. It was Lucy's bathtime.

From the lounge came the sound of gunfire and horses' hooves. She could hear Lucy's soft prattle, and Gary, with all the knowledge of a four-year-old, predicting the outcome of the gunfight.

She wandered through. She glanced at her husband. Ken, she longed to cry, Ken, we're no longer the two young lovers . . . we're growing older and we don't notice the changes.

She wanted to lay her head on his knees and weep quietly for the past and have him comfort her with words and reassurances.

But she could not. Not until the children were in bed, and by that time the moment of her feeling would be gone — swept away amongst pyjamas, bedtime stories and clean vests.

She stood forlornly behind Ken's chair, gazing down at the top of his head. She saw the hair touching the collar of his shirt, the way his glasses rested on his ears. He sat, unable to read his book, as Lucy clambered about his knee and Gary shot him dozens and dozens of questions.

SENSING her presence, Ken reached up behind him for her hand. A gentle squeeze, a gesture somehow absent-minded. Almost, she thought sadly, a habit. *Continued on page 94*

SOOTY — The Little Puss With The Great, Big Heart

SOOTY was really my son Michael's cat, for she surely adored the ground he walked on and he odored her in return. However, my husband, John, was the first to meet Sooty.

A client brought Sooty's mother to our veterinary surgery in Sussex. We learned that the cat had given birth to a litter of malformed kittens in the garden hedge, so her owner decided to bring her in for a check-up to find out if there were more kittens yet to be born.

Upon examination John felt a small lump which he thought could be a placenta, so he gave her an injection to help her expel it.

The end product of two hours of waiting and watching was Sooty, the only perfectly-formed kitten the poor cat ever had.

We decided to keep the cat in overnight to look after her and to give her the necessary injections. So I telephoned the owner to tell her the good news and added that the kitten was a female. I was quite taken aback by her reply, for she said, "Put it to sleep, I don't want it."

I managed to persuade her to keep the kitten until it was weaned by its mother, and then told her that we'd love to have the little one ourselves. At this the owner's attitude completely changed, she said she would be delighted for us to have the kitten, and, of course, she would keep it for us.

So at two weeks old, Sooty, by now a beautiful Persian cross, came to live with us.

Small she may have been, says Veronica Cenco, but Sooty brooked no interference in bringing up her family. Then came that terrible day when we'd no choice but to take over from her . . .

She was a dainty little creature and as the months went by she attached herself more and more to Michael, following him everywhere. He, in turn, thought there was no cat quite like Sooty, and even an unintentional scratch from her very sharp claws brought no rebuke from him.

AT nine months Sooty had her first litter. She gave birth to four beautiful and normal kittens. When she was nearing her time we made a quiet corner ready for her in the dining-room and put her in it. We hoped she'd understand that we wanted her to have her kittens there.

However, when Michael went up to bed, Sooty went upstairs with him as usual.

Soon after Michael had fallen asleep he was awakened by Sooty moving about on his legs. Sitting up to see why she was so restless he was surprised to see she'd already had one kitten. He called me, so I ran upstairs and took Sooty and her kitten downstairs to one of the cages we kept for sick animals. There, within half an hour she had the other three. There was no trouble or fuss, she had

everything under control. Although she made it very plain that the kittens were exclusively for Michael by refusing to let anyone else go near them.

She had two litters a year and then gave herself eight months rest. She made an excellent mother, and was quite a disciplinarian, and wouldn't allow any interference with their upbringing.

Should a kitten step out of line and playfully slap his mother, she wouldn't hesitate to box his ears for his trouble.

Then we decided to emigrate to New Zealand, and the last litter Sooty had in England arrived on Michael's birthday. Something went wrong, however, and only one kitten survived, a female whom we named Venus. So Sooty and her eight-week-old kitten travelled with us to New Zealand.

She settled down remarkably well in her new home and took charge of the garden, making a summer house for herself in the shrubbery at the side of the garden. She also switched her "confinements" to suit the change-round of the seasons.

S OOTY had her last litter the very day Michael came home from boarding school for his May holidays. After making a great fuss of her, he took her and the box with the four babies into his room.

On the sixteenth day, the kittens' eyes were full open.

Sooty, having fed and washed them, pushed the four of them up into a corner on her own toilet. She was most particular about this and washed herself thoroughly and smoothed down her fur, then decided to go outside.

Whilst her kittens were small and so dependent upon her, she never left them for long.

It was then that a terrible thing happened. Sooty was run over as she was hurrying back to her kittens.

Mercifully her death was instantaneous. It is difficult to describe how the family felt. We were all numb with horror and shock that such a dreadful thing could have happened to Sooty and, of course, Michael was quite heartbroken.

At first, John said that perhaps he should put all the kittens to sleep since they were so tiny, but he was well and truly shouted down.

It was up to us to wean the kittens, so I purchased a toy feeding bottle with a teat and made three fairly large holes in it. The bottle held two ounces of liquid, but the kittens
Continued overleaf

93

Continued from previous page
needed four ounces of warm milk each feed.

It was an exhausting task but so rewarding, and our letters to Michael were full of their progress and all the little tricks they got up to.

WHEN they were six weeks old it was time for our monthly visit to see Michael.

It was our intention to take the kittens with us, but the local doctor's wife, Maisie, heard about our plans and begged to be allowed to have the quads for the day.

David, her husband, promised to return them early the following morning, which he did.

A few days later Maisie called with her own cat and asked immediately if the quads were all right. I replied that they appeared to be. She then said that she felt very worried since she thought her cat had picked up cat flu.

I was terribly anxious about our four, especially as the infection can be carried on clothing. Three days later my worst fears were realised, as all the kittens went down with cat flu.

For the next two weeks I stayed with them day and night, and they were dosed daily and injected every three to four hours. Maisie telephoned daily to ask after them, feeling in some way responsible, she said.

Towards the end of the second week we began to see a slight improvement, so I started small feeds of chicken. They became stronger daily, although the two weaker kittens took longer and needed more care, since they were so tiny to begin with.

When two friends asked for a kitten each we let them have the two stronger ones, a tabby and white tom, and a blue, half-Persian female. The other two we kept ourselves and called them "Moosie Boy" and "Dusan."

It took great patience to teach them all they should know, such as how to lap without putting their feet in their food, and to dig a little hole outside for their toilets.

It had been exhausting, but how worth while, and what a joy to watch their funny little antics. Best of all we have a lasting reminder of our dear departed cat, Sooty. ■

Continued from page 91
She stared blindly at the screen.

"Find what you were looking for?" His voice was a low murmur.

"Yes. Yes, they were all bundled together in the attic cupboard, just as you said."

And I found a bit of us there, too, she thought. A bit of us wedged between old programmes and souvenirs . . . and it made me sad . . .

She waited until the credits rolled up the screen, and Gary rolled over on to his stomach, grinning from ear to ear. "I knew it! I knew he'd get shot!"

Gillian plucked Lucy from Ken's knee and headed for the bathroom. She gave the chubby pink body an extra hug as she popped her into the warm water.

Lucy, still baby-fat, with dimpled arms and knees and the smile of an angel. Her lashes, spiky and dark, lay softly against the rosy curve of her cheek.

Lucy, her angelic daughter, with the stubbornness of a mule and a wild temper, which exploded violently, then evaporated just as quickly . . .

Lucy, singing softly to herself, trailed chubby fingers through the water. She clasped her hands together suddenly, holding them secretively to her chest.

Spiky lashes flickered, then blue eyes gazed up at her.

She raised cupped hands to Gillian. "Caught a fish, Mummy," she announced.

Gillian smiled as the ritual of bathtime began again.

IT was later, much later, as she and Ken sat by the fire, that the uneasy feeling caught hold of her again.

She glanced up from her sewing, watching him as he read. He sat, his head slightly to one side, pulling his ear in an absent-minded gesture. The way he sat, the suggestion of a frown on his forehead, were so familiar, yet suddenly the more she looked, so strange!

She laid down her sewing and knelt by his feet in front of the fire.

"Ken —"

"Mmmm?"

He raised his eyebrows, but didn't quite manage to raise his head from the book.

"Ken, why don't we plan something special, just the two of us."

He looked up, taking off his glasses slowly.

"Plan something? Like what?"

She shrugged. "Oh, I don't know. Dinner somewhere . . . Just the two of us. Let's make it just the two of us."

He ruffled her hair.

"Fine," he said. "One day next week? Oh, I'll have to work late on Thursday and Friday — maybe if we left it to the week after —"

"Ken!" She stood up, suddenly exasperated.

"I don't mean next week, the week after, sometime, never!"

Her shoulders drooped. "We never do anything together. If we go out, it's always with Madge and Harry, or in a crowd at the golf club."

Continued on page 98

LAUNCHING OUT

My husband looked slightly exhausted after his maiden voyage, but he told me he'd enjoyed every minute of it. It had been a bit tiring for him as his passengers kept firing questions at him and asking if they could steer the ship.

Still, all in all, his trip was a huge success and he wouldn't have missed it for the world.

And my two grandchildren enjoyed it too, and agreed that Grandad was an excellent skipper — he'd just spent an hour with them on our local boating pond.

"My Hair-Raising Day at

A brand-new hair-do, that's what I promised myself, says Margaret Brown. But after one look at my hair I was sure the stylist was going to give me a real wigging!

I SIMPLY hate going to the hairdresser. In fact, I hate it so much that I hardly ever go. I mean, just sitting there with steadily barbecuing ears and a year-old magazine with all the recipes torn out . . .

Anyway, this morning I actually had time to look at myself in the mirror in quite a leisurely manner, having discovered the bedroom clock was five minutes fast and I

had a time bonus before dashing off to work.

And what, I wondered, was this stuff on top of my head through which I normally draw a rapid comb before covering it up with a headsquare?

Since the last time I had really looked at it, it had sort of changed colour. It was now fairly liberally sprinkled with salt and pepper, and it just hung there as if it had given

Jeremy's"

up all hope — rather like a tired, elderly sheep dog.

Just then my husband poked his head round the bedroom door. "I'm off, dear, and don't forget we're dining out tonight." And with a slam of the front door, he was gone.

Don't forget what, did he say? Dining out? Yes, with Mr and Mrs Somebody-or-other, who were *very* important in the way of business. But how could I possibly face them with a head of hair which wouldn't pass muster as a well-used floor mop?

So I grabbed the telephone directory, and half an hour later I was wondering just where all the hairdressers had gone . . .

THERE were plenty of hair *stylists,* calling themselves in-numerable exotic names, but there wasn't one cosy Rosemary's or Anne's Salon to be seen.

Nervously I decided to give Alfie a call, because he sounded more sort of down to earth than the rest.

"Alfie?" shrilled the supercilious voice at the other end. "Alfie is booked up solid for three months."

Then I tried Heavenly Hair, who snappily told me eight weeks and not a moment before.

Jeremy was engaged, and five minutes later he was *still* engaged. I was just thinking of cutting the whole lot off and saying I was recovering from a mysterious Eastern illness when Jeremy answered at last.

And it turned out I'd got lucky. The engaged call had been — you'll never guess — a cancellation. Yes, a cancellation for Jeremy, and his silky voice betrayed a trace of petulance at the absolute nerve of

it. However, he would see me, in half an hour.

IN fact, "Jeremy's" was disguised as a particularly noisy disco-thèque, and when I finally identified it and slunk in, I felt not just dowdy but positively ancient.

Not a soul appeared to be a day over 17 except Jeremy, who could, at a pinch, be knocking 22. He wore a russet-coloured shirt with a dangling locket, and emerald green trousers. His own long, luxuriant hair shone and bounced like a kitten's.

I sat huddled miserably under the great apron which, despite pounding music and spotlights, is still considered essential for all hair treatments.

My hands wriggled desperately underneath it, trying to find a way out to deal with an itchy nose which always overwhelms me when I'm nervous.

As I struggled, I suddenly became aware of Jeremy standing behind me, looking steadily at me in the mirror. Even more unnerved, I tried a witty remark, but it didn't raise even a glimmer on his handsome features.

He lifted a slight, elegant finger to his lips and it was only then I realised that he wasn't trying to make polite conversation or even indulge in a spot of mirror flirtation. He was contemplating. He was composing and creating. He was considering how to make a silk purse out of a sow's ear.

I finally managed to get my arms free to scratch my nose when, rather reluctantly, he lifted up a handful of my hair and pursed his lips before letting it fall back to my head with a slight thunk, giving away its shocking condition.

"Brian," he called suddenly. "Brian, come over here a moment, will you?" *Continued overleaf.*

G

Continued from previous page

Brian, even younger and terribly good looking, sauntered over.

"What would you do with this, Brian?" Jeremy asked, sounding as if only a miracle could accomplish anything at all.

Brian frowned and said, "What was it like — what colour . . . I mean, before . . . ?"

Before what? Before I had reached the terrible antiquity of 34 years? "Blonde," I grunted. "Well, blondish. With a fringe."

Suddenly, without so much as a "please," I was swivelled around and my neck bent backwards over the basin, and I was shampooed, rinsed and lotioned. Finally released and towel-wrapped, which was all pretty familiar ground so far. There must be more to come, I thought. And there was.

JEREMY stood behind me again, scissors in hand and a look of concentration in his eyes. He snipped here and there and every so often slashed the scissors around so quickly I could hardly follow their progress.

Jeremy called Brian over again and they went into a huddled discussion, and finally Jeremy, grandly brandishing his scissors, withdrew with a gracious smile. The Master had performed the miracle — the apprentice would finish it off.

Brian worked in total silence, blow-drying my hair. Then, apparently satisfied, he called for Jeremy, who trimmed a hair here and there to show he was still the boss.

Cautiously and fearfully I opened one eye and gave my reflection a quick once over. The other eye opened in sheer surprise to help its partner witness the transformation . . .

The sheep dog look had been replaced by short, expertly-cut and tapered hair, soft and shaped. It wasn't me — or was it?

★   ★   ★   ★

"You look sort of different," my husband said as we waited for Mr and Mrs Somebody-or-other. "New dress?"

"No, I had — yes, yes it is. Like it?"

"Yes, very nice," he murmured as he looked at the dress he had given me two Christmases before.

I've already made another appointment with Jeremy — bless his beautiful fingers! ∎

Continued from page 95

She knelt in front of him. "I want *us* to do something special, the way we used to do, in the beginning."

He looked at her for a moment.

"All right. Although," he said thoughtfully, "where you'll get a babysitter for those two terrors at short notice . . ."

She sighed, beaten. "I know, I know." She stood up, restlessly wrapping her arms about her.

"Why is it like a military operation every time we want to go anywhere?"

She whirled round, her eyes sparkling. "That's it!" She kissed the tip of his nose. "We'll stay at home. I'll get the kids in bed early tomorrow, and we'll have a special meal, candles, the lot!"

Ken polished his glasses. "Yes," he said, warming to the idea. "I'll get a bottle of wine, treat myself to a couple of good cigars."

Then he looked at her closely, suddenly dubious.

"I haven't forgotten an anniversary or a birthday, have I?" he asked hesitantly.

"No . . . But why should we need a reason to celebrate? Let's just be nice to ourselves!"

She looked at him, wanting to tell him about the diary, but now it seemed silly. The sharpness of the feeling she'd had had gone.

She picked up pen and paper and sat on the settee, planning her menu. She chewed the end of the pen, juggling with the housekeeping money, her spirits rising. Perhaps it was as easy as this to recapture those days when they'd only had time for each other . . .

SHE took twice as long as usual to go round the supermarket next day.

She chose a melon. They were expensive, but an easy first course. She wandered over to the butcher's section and lingered over her choice of steaks. She bought mushrooms and salad greens, tossing them into the trolley with gay abandon. She'd decided to make a meringue shell for the sweet, filled with fresh cream and strawberries.

Finally, the trolley laden, she manoeuvred Gary and Lucy through the check-out and loaded the groceries into the car.

Brushing back a wisp of hair from her eyes, she slammed the boot shut, and on an impulse took the children across to the café for ice-cream sundaes.

After all, she thought as she stirred her coffee and watched them tuck in, they would have to have their share of the celebration, too.

IN A STEW!

My husband loves his tea very strong and black, and criticises any brew which does not come up to his expectations.

It used to embarrass me whenever we were in a café or restaurant.

But at last I've found the answer.

Now I have the first cup. Then, when the waitress turns her back, I transfer two or three tea-bags from my handbag to the pot and give them a good stir.

The resulting obnoxious stew pleases my husband and lets me enjoy my own cuppa in peace — although I shudder to think what the kitchen staff think!

Half an hour later they emerged from the café into the sunny square. Lucy, a chocolate moustache over her top lip, was ready for her morning nap. Taking a firm grip of two hands, Gillian led them back to the car.

She gave a longing look towards the hairdressers'. It would have been nice if she'd had her hair done, she thought suddenly. But there was never enough time, never enough money!

But nothing could dampen her spirits, and the three of them drove home to a rousing version of "The Grand Old Duke Of York." She felt organised and capable.

WHILE Ken read the children a bedtime story, Gillian set to work on the meringue shell. It would have to cook while they were eating, but it would be safe enough, she thought. She had meant to do it earlier . . .

She checked on the baked potatoes, and popped the steaks, mushrooms and tomatoes under a low grill. The melon, cubed and ready, was in the fridge.

She tapped a finger against her chin, and glanced at her watch. She only had to slip upstairs to change her dress and that would be that. She congratulated herself. She had really been extraordinarily efficient!

When she came down again, Ken was opening the wine. The rich, heavy smell of cigar smoke lingered in the room.

He handed her a small box. She took it, fingering it, exclaiming, looking at him questioningly.

"Open it," he said.

It was a tiny silver locket, beautifully patterned, perfect in its smallest detail.

"But why?" she asked, as she fastened the chain round her neck.

"Lots of things," he said, drawing her into his arms, and talking into her hair. "For the times I've been grumpy at breakfast, or forgotten to kiss you . . ." He squeezed her. "You know."

She smiled, a little wobbly smile, fingering the locket.

They sat down at the table, tasted the wine, and Ken lit the candles on the table.

The food was nice, Gillian had to admit, as she tucked into her steak. Ken put his finger and thumb together and kissed them in appreciation. "Marvellous! Why should we go out for a meal when you cook like this?"

Gillian slipped her shoes off and wiggled her toes.

"It is nice, isn't it?"

He touched her hand and leaned forward.

She wondered, as she looked into his eyes, if he knew the silly reasons behind the meal, and suddenly, there was time to tell him, knowing he would understand.

She twirled her wineglass and started to speak . . .

THEN Gary, in rumpled pyjamas, his hair spiky and his face flushed from sleep, peered at them from the doorway.

'Why is it dark in here, Mummy?"

Gillian watched their evening crumble away from their grasp and bit back the words that would never be said . . .

She held her arms out.

"It's candlelight, silly, It's not dark. Don't you think it's pretty?"

He came to her, leaning against her, still dazed from sleep.

She pushed his hair back from his forehead. "Why aren't you asleep?"

"Couldn't. I had a nightmare. I want to stay up with you and Daddy."

BETTE DAVIS

★ ★ ★ ★ ★ ★ ★ ★ ★ ★ ★ ★ ★ ★

❝ "I have eyes like a bullfrog, a neck like an ostrich and limp hair. You have to be good to survive with that equipment." ❞

★ ★ ★ ★ ★ ★ ★ ★ ★ ★ ★ ★

He peered at the table, his interest increasing with wakefulness. "Lucy's awake, too," he added. "I heard her talking to her teddy."

As if on cue, they heard Lucy's outraged wail. Ken pushed his chair back. "I'll try to settle her."

Five minutes later, he appeared apologetically at the door, Lucy's arms entwined around his neck.

"She's wide awake, I'm afraid."

Gillian watched as Gary, by this time perched on her knee, helped polish off the remains of her mushrooms.

They rearranged the table and Gillian divided the meringue dessert amongst the four of them.

Absently, she wiped a blob of cream from Lucy's nose, and Ken caught hold of her hand.

"All right?"

She looked into his eyes and saw he was disappointed. Not for himelf, she realised, with a sudden flash of understanding, but for her. He was disappointed because she'd wanted so much for this evening. .

He'd gone along with her idea, though he had no need, she knew now, to prove to himself that they were still together . . .

She didn't want to be the girl in the diary, any more than she wanted Ken to be the boy she'd once known. She looked at the two shiny heads of blonde hair. They'd come a long way since then.

She looked at Ken over the top of Lucy's head and smiled, a long, slow smile, as she felt a delicious rush of happiness. There would be other times when she felt they were somehow separated. But they would survive the sacrifices and the misunderstandings. They were stronger now, sure of each other. And she felt the resentment slip from her shoulders.

Ken had understood, more than she had. And as she saw the answering warmth of his smile, she felt at peace.

They finished the meal slowly. A sticky, noisy, messy meal that was somehow very, very precious.

———— ✳ **THE END** ✳ ————

"I'VE NEVER YOU—"

That's what he was telling her — this man who, five years ago had left her to marry someone else.

Complete Story by

C. B. PIPER

A HAND shot from the car and grabbed her wrist. Evelyn Maxwell gasped and clutched her handbag tighter, imagination flying wildly from robbery to murder.

Then a man's voice said, "Sorry," and she was released. In that second she hadn't even looked at her attacker — now that she was free, she didn't want to. Her heart was thudding. All she wanted was to get away quickly.

"Evelyn," the voice said, and she was shaken to hear her name. Her reaction changed to anger. What sort of game was this?

The car door opened and the man emerged. With shock and disbelief she recognised him.

"Harry! What an idiotic thing to do!" she burst out.

"I'm sorry."

"Sorry? You nearly frightened me to death! Then you could have told the police you were sorry! You haven't grown up much in five years, have you?"

"I have, you know," he replied solemnly.

"You could have fooled me." She was too angry for originality.

FORGOTTEN

"I didn't expect to see you," he said.

"I didn't expect to see *you* either — but if I had I wouldn't have tried to shock you out of your wits."

"Well." He looked very apologetic. "Are you all right now?"

"I suppose so." She still felt ungracious.

"You see," he went on, "suddenly seeing you like that took me by surprise. I was afraid you'd be gone before I could speak to you. It was instinctive to try to stop you."

"At your age you should have learned to curb your instincts," she said. "Fool." She wondered if there was anyone else in the world she could speak to that way after a gap of five years. But there wasn't — only Harry.

"Do you live round here?" he asked.

"In the area." She wasn't going to give him any more information. There was a long pause.

"You're fine." He wasn't asking, she knew. He was taking it for granted, as he always had done with everything.

"I'm all right. But, look, Harry, I really must go now."

Evelyn wasn't simply paying lip-service. She was afraid that if she stayed here talking, Harry would reinstate himself in her mind, or more importantly, in her heart. And she didn't want that. Five years was a lot of days. Sixteen hundred days away from him surely meant she was safe. And she was, she told herself fiercely. Completely safe. She just wanted to get away, that was all.

"Are you happy?" he asked. He wasn't gripping her wrist any more, but he might as well have been.

"Very, thank you. And you ?"

"Idyllically."

"Good." She should be pleased that he was happy. Despite everything, even he was allowed to be happy — but not to the point of being idyllic, surely . . .

"What are you doing here?" she asked.

"Waiting for my wife."

"I hope she won't be long."

"I never met your husband," he said.

"I never met your wife."

"Well, why don't we all have dinner together?"

"Lovely." She smiled doubtfully. "Give me a ring, Harry. The number's in the book."

"I don't know the name," he reminded her.

"Mrs Alastair Maxwell, that's me."

"It suits you," he said. There was another pause, then suddenly he asked, "Evelyn, have you got any children?"

"No." She looked at him defiantly. If he dared to look sympathetic . . .

"Neither have we," he said.

"Oh." She relaxed, the resentment disappearing. Suddenly she wasn't in quite such a rush. "Why haven't you?" she asked.

He smiled wryly. "Anthea declares that to bring children into this world is immoral."

"That's a point," Evelyn said.

"Maybe." He didn't look convinced. "And you?"

She flushed. "I can't have them."

H E looked at her. "I'm sorry. How does Alastair feel?"
"He's very good about it."

"Charitable."

"It's not easy for a man."

"I know," he said shortly.

"Did you want them badly?" she asked.

"Yes."

"So did I," she said.

"Why don't you adopt?" Harry asked her.

"Alastair wants his own or nothing." She hesitated. "Why don't you and Anthea adopt, then? That's not bringing children into the world — it's helping those who are here already."

"I'd like to," Harry said. "Anthea won't."

"Funny we should end up in the same boat," she said.

"We didn't," he retorted. "I wish we had."

Evelyn heard footsteps approaching. "That must be your wife. Goodbye," she said, and moved away so quickly that he had no time to say anything more.

When she got home, Evelyn looked at herself in the mirror. Her cheeks were flushed. That's silly, she thought. Seeing Harry had been fun — but it shouldn't have been that good. It might mean something then — better to mean nothing at all.

She was still sparkling when Alastair came home.

"You're very bright," he said.

"Have you had a good day?" she asked.

Alastair looked a bit vague. "Yes, I suppose so. Yes — definitely. Five firm sales, anyway."

"Five. Oh, Alastair, that's fantastic! We must celebrate. Let's go out to dinner."

"Darling," he said. "Let's stay in — I'm exhausted."

"Oh, all right." Disappointed, Evelyn went to the kitchen to prepare the dinner.

DEAD FUNNY

I used to work for a hot-tempered lawyer who refused to answer phone calls when coping with the morning mail. One day it rang continuously while he was dictating a complicated document.

"Tell whoever it is that I'm out," he roared into the receiver. "Tell him I'm ill! Tell him —" he spluttered with mounting exasperation " — tell him I'm dead!"

But the caller had already been connected. "Sorry to hear the news, Willie," he sympathised. "When's your funeral?"

EIGHT days later Harry phoned. Evelyn hadn't really expected he would, but the idea of the dinner party was quite fun. She admitted to herself that she was curious about Anthea. Doubtless Harry felt the same way about Alastair.

Well, Alastair would surely impress him. Charming, clearly successful, a man who adored her and provided her with everything she wanted . . . nearly. Yes, Harry would have to be impressed.

Except that trying to impress Harry was like trying to draw a line on water. He formed his own opinions and once formed they didn't change.

As she listened she waited for the suggested dinner date. Harry asked how she was, how Alastair was, what she was doing . . . and would she lunch with him that day.

"I can't," she said instinctively. Somehow it was unsafe. Dinner with Anthea and Alastair there would be quite different.

"Are you working?" Harry asked.

"Not exactly."

"No children . . . you said so."

"All right," she said tightly. "So what?"

"So you're free." Harry chuckled at the other end of the line.

"We've got the gas man coming," she lied wildly.

"Not true."

Evelyn sighed. If she accepted Harry's invitation the dangerous prospect of nostalgia loomed high. If she refused . . .

"What do you do with your time, Evelyn?" Harry asked.

"I run an employment agency."

"Then why aren't you at work?"

"My partner and I take alternate days," she told him.

"So you're not bored?"

"Far from it." She smiled. Alastair's business and social life frequently merged. Entertaining foreign buyers, going abroad to exhibitions with him. Life was fun. Life was fine.

"You're not bored, but today you're free?" Harry was saying.

"Yes." Reluctantly.

"Then meet me?"

She hesitated and he laughed. "You haven't far to go, you know. I'm looking at your house right now."

Her head jerked round in alarm and she looked through the window at the call box across the street.

Yes, there was someone in it. And, yes, there was Harry's car.

"Really!" she said. "You're impossible."

"Correct. And you're coming, aren't you?"

She sighed. "Yes, Harry, I'm coming."

"I'll be right over," he said. But she stopped him. For some reason she didn't like the idea of his coming to the flat.

She put on her coat, glanced in the hall mirror and hurried to the lift.

"We're going to . . ."

"A little place you know," she finished for him.

"Clever girl. And wrong! We're going to a little place I *don't* know."

"Oh. Experimental?"

"In a way. I've been told about it. It should suit our purpose perfectly." He winked.

Evelyn looked at him sideways. "You make it sound very secretive."

Harry just grinned at her.

THE restaurant was small, cheerful and expensive. They had a drink first then ordered the meal. Evelyn wasn't hungry — but she was a little nervous. Harry wasn't hungry either, but they went through the formalities and both ended up ordering Dover Sole.

"You still like fish," he observed.

"You promised it would give me brains," she replied. "I'm still trying for them."

Then quite suddenly, with no preliminary, he said, "Evelyn, I did love you."

She was shaken. She had been prepared for nostalgia, even mild flirtation, but this was direct and unwelcome.

"You knew that anyway, didn't you?" he went on.

"I suppose so."

"You suppose?"

"All right. I did," she said sharply.

"Well? Aren't you going to say something?"

She raised her glass. "Cheers."

"Evelyn, you loved me too. Aren't you going to say so?"

"Harry." She was angry at being made uneasy. "What good could it possibly do?"

"I'd just like to hear it."

"That's nonsense. You know how we felt. It fizzled out, that's all."

"Did it? Is that how it ended?"

AS GOOD AS GOLD

I wonder what young couples getting married today would think of the wedding present I received.

It was during the last war and food rationing was very strict. A friend on leave from the Merchant Navy brought us a rare gift. We were delighted, and so were our friends, when we shared our treasure.

It had pride of place at our reception. We hadn't been given diamonds or rubies, though — just four large Spanish onions!

"Yes," she said positively. "Not with a bang, but with a whimper."

" 'This is the way the world ends' . . . It did for me, Evelyn."

"That's not true, Harry, and five years later I should have thought you'd have learned a lot more sense. Why try to stir up ashes that are as dead as . . ."

"Don't say mutton. It wouldn't sound right."

"Well, why anyway?"

"I don't know. Perhaps I'm looking for a little security."

"Security?" Evelyn laughed incredulously. "Harry, wherever you look for it, you won't find it with me. You seem secure enough, anyway."

"Do I?" He looked directly at her.

"Certainly," she said, but she wasn't too sure he was.

"Good," he said. "I'm glad it looks that way. Are you happy, Evelyn?"

"I am. Idyllically." She used the word defiantly, remembering how

Continued on page 110

We Shared Our Home With

It was the home we'd dreamed of for years, says Mrs Dorothy Campbell. But we hadn't bargained for the mysterious lodger who turned our dream into a nightmare.

WE were such a happy family when we moved from lodgings into a brand new house, twenty-five years ago. Though we were very hard up, the move meant the freedom of a garden for my three-year-old daughter, and her little sister, only three weeks old. And, of course, it also meant the security of our own key to the front door.

Our happiness increased over the years as we gradually obtained the extra furniture that made our house into a home. It took at least eight years of hardship and scrimping to do it, but it was worth it when at last all the rooms were papered, painted and reasonably furnished. And, to complete our joy, that was the time our son was born.

All went well for two more years then strange things began to happen when my husband was out at night. With an extra mouth to feed, we had to have more money, so he had taken a job involving night shift.

My younger daughter, then eight years old and prone to sleep-walking, often came downstairs, but I just turned her round along the passage and led her back up to her bed.

One night, though, when I was sitting reading, I heard a creak on the stairs and the sound of footsteps along the passage. I thought it must be my daughter again but when I opened the sitting-room door no-one was there. I went upstairs to my daughters' bedroom and found both girls fast asleep.

I decided I must have been imagining things but from then on life became a nightmare. I noticed lights were switched on, when I was sure I'd switched them off, and I heard sounds of footsteps and furniture being moved.

The strange thing was that the noises didn't occur when my daughters and husband were around.

However, I was worried, and we decided to get a dog.

For a while, the disturbances stopped, but I was still unhappy.

Then, one night after the children were in bed, things began to happen again. The dog jumped up, ran to the front door of the room and suddenly

can **you** explain it?

108

A Ghost

seemed to freeze with his hair standing up on end.

Once again, I heard the footsteps across the landing, then down the stairs. This time I really was scared. Armed with a poker, I crept round the passage but again no-one was there.

The dog started to howl and the children, who this time had heard the footsteps too, came downstairs and I tried to reassure them.

Now everyone believed that there was something strange about the house. But although "the ghost" frightened us, it didn't seem to bear malice and we came to no harm.

AS the years went on, we called our mysterious lodger "Stan", and even when it threw things about, we learned to live with it.

Once the girls had grown up and married, my husband and I did what I'd wanted to do for years — moved to a smaller house.

The night before we moved, everything was packed, my husband was at work and my son and I were watching television. The night was warm and still. But suddenly the doors upstairs crashed shut, windows banged, wind howled around the rooms and the dog went berserk.

Terrified, we ran out of the front door around to our neighbours.

Our neighbour went round to our house, looked everywhere, and found nothing.

Next day, as our furniture was moved out, to make room for the new occupants, I breathed a sigh of relief.

A few weeks after settling into our new house, I was passing the old one when the woman who now lived there saw me and called me over. She handed me a photo which her husband had found under the floorboards on the stair landing, when he'd put in the central heating.

"It must be yours," she said, "You were the first people in this house."

I looked at the photo, but it wasn't of anyone we knew. It was a wartime wedding photo. The 'groom was a Naval officer, and the couple had a guard of honour of Naval men. The date was on the back — 1943.

But the house wasn't built till 1950!

I sent the photo to the local papers, asking if anyone could solve the mystery, but I had no answers. I kept the photo for two months, but I couldn't stop looking at it. Finally, I burnt it.

The mystery is still unsolved. Was Stan looking for the photo? Or was perhaps someone murdered on the site of our old house?

Whatever it was, we'll probably never find out. ∎

Continued from page 107
he'd used it before.

"Lucky old us," Harry said. "We're both idyllically happy."

"Good."

"And both liars."

Evelyn twisted her glass in her hands. "Harry, what game are you playing?"

"I'm not playing, Evelyn. I want you back!"

SHE smiled. "At least you're direct about it."

"Why not?"

"What about old-fashioned marriage vows? And obligations? And love? Ever heard of them?"

"I've heard of love." Harry's voice was bitter. "Anthea and I are finished anyway."

"Does she know?"

"We both do."

"So you're looking for someone to bolster up the old ego. And, conveniently, I happened to appear. You've still got the cheek of the devil, Harry."

"No, Evelyn. I'm deadly serious. Don't think it's just because I saw you last week. It didn't fizzle out, Evelyn. You left me."

"Harry, we wanted different things. It ended with arguments and a lot of bad feeling . . ."

He looked hurt. "That's not true!"

"It is. You were a womaniser."

"And you wouldn't say 'yes' to marriage!"

"What? Look, I'm sorry, Harry, but I think the wires are crossed."

"I wanted you to marry me."

"But you just forgot to mention it, right?"

"I wouldn't have behaved as I did if you'd been more enthusiastic."

"So which came first, the chicken or the egg?"

"Oh, so you accuse me of going out with other women because I got nowhere with you?"

"Yes! And I'm right, too!" She was blazing. "Now do you believe me? There are no ashes left to stir."

"No. They're dead — as mutton."

The grilled sole looked delicious, but they picked at it. Harry ordered white wine. Evelyn said she didn't want any.

"Honestly," he said, "you're an infuriating woman!"

"And you're an arrogant man! Poor Anthea . . ."

"And heaven help Alastair."

"Don't waste your sympathy on Alastair. He's fine. And I love him!"

Harry looked at her gloomily. "Then why are you having lunch with me?"

"Sheer curiosity." She was relieved to discover it was true.

"This wasn't a good idea, then?"

"No."

"Pity. What about that dinner? The four of us?"

"Forget it."

Suddenly, very softly, he said, "Evelyn, can't you love me again? I need you. I mean it."

"Harry, it's been over for years."

"No. It's been on my mind for years."

"That must have been a good basis for your marriage."

"See me again?"

"No."

"Evelyn . . ." He took her hand. "Don't try to fool me. We still attract each other, whatever you pretend. We could still love each other . . ."

She pulled away her hand and with difficulty resisted the impulse to slap his face. The look she gave him withered the rest of the meal to silence.

"I'll take you home," he said finally.

"Thank you."

THAT evening when Alastair came home, Evelyn was not, as she usually was, in the kitchen. She was relaxed in the sitting-room, with a drink beside her. There were fresh glasses and some dishes of nuts and olives. She was wearing a dress she knew he liked. She knew, too, that she looked exceptionally pretty.

"You look gorgeous," Alastair said. "Anything special?" He nodded to her drink.

Continued overleaf

☆☆☆☆☆☆☆☆☆☆☆☆☆☆☆☆☆☆☆☆☆☆☆☆☆☆☆

JOHNNY WEISSMULLER

★★★★★★★★★★★★★★★★★★★★★★★★★★★★★

According to Johnny Weissmuller, the greatest screen Tarzan of them all, he landed the rôle by accident. He called at the film studio to visit Clark Gable, who was a friend of his, but found that the guard at the gate wouldn't let him in. Then someone mentioned that they were auditioning for Tarzan. The guard agreed to let him in if he went to the screen test, and so Weissmuller joined 70 or so other hopefuls. He got the job!

★★★★★★★★★★★★★★★★★★★★★★★★★★★★★

Continued from previous page

"Yes. I'm just waiting to go out to dinner."

He was startled. "Oh? Where?"

"I'm being taken to The Oasis Restaurant."

"The Oasis? That used to be our place. I haven't taken you in years. Why didn't you tell me?"

"I'm telling you now."

It was obvious Alastair was uneasy. "Who are you going with?" he asked uncertainly.

"A man," she said. "Someone I'm in love with."

"Evelyn, what are you saying?" She heard the jealousy and disbelief in his voice.

She came and put her arms round his neck. "I'm going with *you*, darling."

"*What?*"

"Do you know why we haven't been to The Oasis for so long?"

"Tell me."

"Because we've let our careers take over our personal lives. There's room for both, but especially there's room for us. We've only got each other. We *need* each other. I've suddenly realised."

"I don't understand." Alastair's voice was puzzled.

"I don't expect you to, darling. Call it woman's nonsense, sentiment — a warning, if you like. All I know is I love you. Do you realise we've been in danger of letting love fly out of the window — just because we're used to it?

"Let's live while we can, Alastair. We've almost forgotten how to look at each other as people!"

"I haven't forgotten how to look at you as a person, Evelyn," he said. "That's why I've been so distracted lately. Wary, too. I've watched you — first bright, then suddenly sort of deflated. I've worked myself into the ground and you've got prettier and sadder."

She looked at him uncomprehendingly. He put his hand under her chin and lifted her face to his. "Darling, before I go and change I want to say something. For months I've been worrying. I've argued with myself, put up barriers, crashed them down. Finally, I've . . . Evelyn, do you still want us to adopt a baby?"

She looked at him incredulously, then, speechless, flung her arms round his neck. She felt her tears on his shirt.

"Don't cry, love," he said softly. "You look so pretty. Don't spoil it."

"Spoil it?" She smiled at him through the tears. "Oh, Alastair, I love you. You're so very special!"

"Special?" He smiled. "You mean I'm me. I'm not just any old Tom, Dick or Harry?"

She looked at him, loving him. "Darling," she laughed, half-sobbing, "you've just put it in a nutshell. The one thing you certainly are not is any Tom or Dick — or Harry!" □

—————— * **THE END** * ——————

Complete Story by
DOROTHY L. GARRARD

That SPECIAL WHISTLE

— He'd taught her it, but she'd have to practise pretty hard before he'd come running!

"B AY!" I called across the park, where a few dogs were running free. "Bay! Here!"

He took no notice, of course, but the stranger I could see out of the corner of my eye watched with interest.

Bay's full name was Bayard de Rousseau Chavlon, and I took him out for walks every day. He had the supercilious expression of a camel, and looked like a hearth-rug slung over a clothes line. He was, in fact, an Afghan hound, and belonged to my neighbour, Mrs Connington.

Originally, he'd been owned by her husband, who used to enter him for shows, perhaps that partly accounted for his expression. However, as Mr Connington had died over a year ago, and as Mrs Connington was old and frail, she hadn't the physical strength to take him out for exercise.

I was fond of Mrs Connington; she'd been like a granny to me. Years back we'd baked gingerbread men in her kitchen, all cosy and smug, and she'd helped me conquer the intricacies of crochet, saving yours truly, Jean Morton, from being bottom of the needlework class.

So I could do no other than help out when the old lady wanted to keep Bayard for her late husband's sake. Unfortunately, neither Bayard nor I cared for the arrangement much. Though I was quite tall, he managed to look me in the eye disdainfully, as if he were my equal in every way — and was doing *me* a favour.

H

As a rule, he was reasonably obedient — after the inevitable pause for thought. Perhaps some canine sixth sense told him he'd better not try me too far, or his life at Bilton Crescent might come to an abrupt end.

Bayard liked Parkside — there were long stretches of rough grass which flew satisfyingly under his dish-mop paws, sizeable clumps of trees to be "investigated" and the odd alien beast to be chased. Above all, he could get well away from me, delaying his return home, indefinitely, by a remarkable display of deafness.

At the moment he was having an acute attack of independence. The watching stranger came nearer.

He casually addressed the park in general, and me in particular, since I was the only person within earshot.

"It's really advisable to train a dog thoroughly before allowing it to roam over such a large area."

I was already late — again — for a date with Jeff, and somewhat fraught. Jeff Lord was the most exciting thing that had happened to me since adolescence, tall and blond, a very desirable property locally. That he should have singled me out for attention was a small miracle in itself, and I had neither the beauty nor the personality to get away with being constantly late.

"Bay's not mine," I answered the stranger. "He's the dog opposite."

"Dog opposite?"

"Opposite me — my home," I explained impatiently.

He grinned. It was a fetching kind of grin, if you were susceptible to grins — which I wasn't at the moment. Not from know-it-all strangers, anyway.

"Well, opposite seems to be a good name for him."

"He's well trained. He can be perfectly obedient when he wants to."

He laughed, a little disbelievingly, I thought. "Can't we all!"

"He was a show dog, until his owner died," I said testily. "He had to be obedient, or he'd never have won all those cups."

"What's his name again?"

I told him — the full works. When his eyebrows shot up I was rather pleased it was so impressive.

Then I realised that Bay had vanished again.

B AY!" I called at the top of my voice, feeling that I could cheerfully have strangled that dog with his own tail.

"Try his full name," the stranger suggested solemnly. He was laughing and I didn't find the situation amusing. I gave him a withering glance.

He pursed his lips and emitted a strange, two-toned whistle, with a kind of trill in the middle of it.

"What's that supposed to be?" I asked sarcastically. "An irresistible whistle?"

He gave me a long look that would have made my toes curl, if my

A Shaggy Dog Story

IT was a grey, wet day and the rain clearly depressed everybody on the bus. I sat on the top deck — which was fairly full — and stared out of the window . . . while most of the other passengers hid behind their newspapers.

Then another passenger came upstairs to join us — a four-legged one!

He was a large shaggy mongrel, who went straight to the front of the bus, sat down and looked out.

The odd thing was — nobody came upstairs with him! Ah, well, I thought, his owner will be downstairs.

When the conductor came upstairs to collect the fares, he spotted the dog and pushed his hat to the back of his head.

"You again!" he said — and all of us turned to stare from him to the dog, who looked blandly back at the conductor and wagged his tail in the friendliest way.

The conductor shook his head. "Every time it rains," he said, "you sneak on my bus for a free trip home — all nice and dry!"

He stooped and patted the dog, then went on to collect the fares. Minutes later, he stopped, glanced out of window and belled the driver.

"Your stop!" he called, and the dog was off down the stairs as nice as you please.

As the bus moved on, the conductor grinned. "One of these days the inspector's going to catch him!"

For the rest of the journey, I noticed there was a smile on everyone's face.

All thanks to a smart dog who was smart enough to cadge a free lift . . . and a conductor who had the warmth to let himself be taken a loan of.

A small incident — but how it brightened a dull winter day.

feet hadn't already been stamping with frustration.

I wished I hadn't been quite as sarcastic, and I blushed, despite myself. He looked at me again, and I noticed his brown eyes under his crinkly hair — good looking, if I hadn't been too annoyed to be influenced by that sort of thing.

"That's a whistle you should practise," he said. "It has an irresistible attraction —" my face was scarlet now "— for dogs," he finished, gazing thoughtfully at my fiery cheeks.

Fortunately, his attention was diverted then by the sight of Bayard approaching, head high, body swaying, his feet flattening the frosty grass in dignified rhythm. A short way behind him I saw that something else was clearing a path, but since the grass was longish I couldn't quite make out what it was.

Bay halted in front of the stranger, gave him an inscrutable once-

Continued on page 118

The Cheeky
Took Over

Tiny, frail eyes not yet open, I had doubts that Sam would survive, says Mrs J. Morgan. But our helpless "baby" had very different ideas of his own . . .

LIVING in the country with three children, I have become used to having various small creatures, usually birds, brought to me with instructions to mend their wings, legs or just to keep them alive.

However, I was shattered when, one day, the children came running in with three tiny, wrinkled, blind and really rather nasty-looking creatures. Upon being told that they were baby squirrels that had fallen out of the nest, my first reaction was to tell the children to put them back where they had found them! Apparently this was impracticable, and so began the long struggle to see if we could rear them.

Obviously the squirrels were very young, and needed food and warmth straightaway. My husband made a tiny bottle for them to drink out of and fixed up a box with a lamp underneath to keep them warm.

By now, the children were deciding which should be their own particular pet. Graham chose his and called him The Virginian, Carol's was Little Joe and Robert, who chose the biggest, declared he was Hoss. Any more unsuitable names would have been hard to choose!

The next thing was to arrange a better system of feeding, so I was despatched to the chemist to ask for a squirrel feeding bottle! As you can imagine, this caused a hilarious reaction, but once the laughter died down I bought a medicine dropper. I also bought glucose and baby cereal for extra nourishment.

In the first few days the little squirrels seemed to be growing, albeit rather slowly. Then suddenly one died. Hardly had the children got over this shock when, a week or so later, another followed him.

This only left us with Hoss. Happily, he was thriving, having by now grown a good coat of fur, and opened his eyes.

Somehow, about this time, we changed his name to Sam Squirrel, rather to

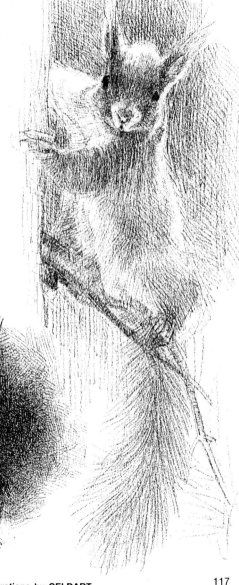

Little Squirrel Who
Our Lives

Robert's annoyance, but when people came to the house and heard me talking about Hoss, I had some very strange looks!

By this time, too, about six weeks after we had found him, Sam had to have a bigger cage. We made one for him, but even so, we could see that he wanted to be let out.

At first we let him in the house for short periods, when he would play like a kitten and run and jump from one person to another, or take great leaps across the furniture.

He was also eating different things — in fact, he would try to eat everything he found, including the legs of the dining-chairs!

Neighbours often brought him
Continued overleaf

Illustrations by GELDART

Continued from previous page

sugar lumps and nuts, which he loved, and sometimes fruit, which he would take to his special place on the window-sill. There he'd hold it up in his paws and eat it carefully, spitting out the skins and pips for me to clear up!

About this time, when he was spending most of his time indoors, he began making nests and would heave and struggle with great heaps of paper or material and fill up the pockets of coats that were hanging up. We never knew where anything might turn up, he was such a hoarder.

Sam talked a good deal, too. He'd grunt when pleased, but when bed-time came he would defiantly chatter loudly all the way to his cage. Once in, however, he would eat his bed-time porridge, snuggle down in his old woolly jumper and go to sleep at once.

He was soon about three-quarters grown, and we realised we would soon have to let him go to find his own way, so we started by taking him into the garden for a trip up the apple tree.

This was a great success, greeted by much loud chatter and a great show of acrobatics.

The only problem was getting him down again! In the end, I enticed him down with a special favourite, a black cherry, but he was obviously not happy indoors after that, and one day while the door was open he must have scuttled out.

We saw him around for a day or two afterwards. He looked so happy, gliding between the branches in the tree nearby, that it was some con-solation to the children, who, it must be said, missed Sam Squirrel a good deal more than Sam Squirrel missed them!

By now I expect he is a parent, or even a grandparent, himself, and happily living in the wild as he should be. However, he'll always have a place in our hearts — Sam, the friendly, intelligent little squirrel who came to stay. ■

🐿 *personality pets* 🐿 *personality pets* 🐿

Continued from page 115

over, then arranged himself tidily alongside, waiting regally for his leash to be attached. He'd never done that for me in his life.

I moved towards him, and he backed off.

The stranger held out his hand for the leash with a satisfied expression and, if it hadn't been for Jeff, I wouldn't have given in so easily. Fuming, I handed it over.

A fluffy wriggling bundle fawned round my ankles, investigating my boots with a black button nose and a small pink tongue. From within the bundle of silky white fur, two bright black eyes gleamed at me.

"She's taken to you," said Bay's "friend," surprised.

Suddenly, I sensed vulnerability. I looked interestedly from midget to man.

"This . . . is *yours?*"

Whatever Bay's faults, he was a dog-sized dog. Nothing, I thought, looked more ridiculous than a tall man with a minute pet. Happily, I watched his complacent expression crack.

"What's her name?"

"Blossom . . ."

It was so unexpected, coming from masculine lips, that I burst out laughing. He was definitely embarrassed now.

"No wonder you prefer to whistle." I laughed.

Yes, it was rude, and certainly out of character for me. But I was so pleased to have turned the tables that I didn't stop to think.

He picked Blossom up.

She looked more like a powder-puff than a flower, and in other circumstances I'd have said she was cute. As it was, I casually accepted Bay's leash and walked away, trying to disguise the fact that he was pulling in the other direction, and all but taking me with him.

SITTING beside Jeff in the cinema, the more I remembered of the encounter in the park, the more uncomfortable I felt. Poor little Blossom! It hadn't been her fault. I hoped she hadn't thought I was laughing at *her* . . .

Jeff's arm moved along the back of my seat, brushed my shoulder and subtly pressed it. Lost in thought, I was startled to see sleek fair hair where dark crinkles should be, and I drew back sharply. Astonished at this unprecedented occurrence, so did Jeff.

"Whatever's the matter, Jean?" Usually he called me Jeannie.

"I'm sorry — I was thinking of something else."

His astonishment increased. "When I'm with you, I can't possibly think of anything else," he murmured reproachfully.

Normally, I lapped up this soulful romantic dialogue, but all at once it sounded as artificial as the drama unfolding on the cinema screen. Why had I been rushing round like a mad thing, offending people, in order to sit here in a stuffy cinema?

I thought of the starlit night outside. "Let's go out," I said.

We strolled past Parkside. I looked up at the trees silhouetted against the stars and suddenly there was one question I had to ask him. "If you had a dog, Jeff, what kind would you choose?"

"I wouldn't," Jeff said simply. "I don't like animals at all — inconvenient and smelly, quite apart from the fact that the hound you take out always makes you late. Besides, he never does as you tell him."

"Only because he thinks I've no right to order him about," I answered, with a flash of insight. "He's a one-man dog."

"Why doesn't the old lady get a paid dog walker?" Jeff grumbled. "Treating you like a hired help . . ."

"It isn't like that at all," I argued. "Mrs Connington is a friend, you know that."

"All I know is, it's that dog's fault you keep me waiting around. I hate people being late."

He also hated anyone to argue with him, but, stubbornly, I went on.

"I'm sorry about that, Jeff, but I can't possibly let Mrs Connington down. She's always been so good to me — and Bay needs lots of exercise."

Jeff halted and turned me masterfully towards him.

"I think it's time you made a choice, once and for all, Jean. That dog — or me."

Jeff obviously thought there was only one possible choice. Not only did I disillusion him, I added insult to injury by not even hesitating.

"Then obviously it'll have to be Bay," I retorted. "Old loyalties come first."

It was a peculiar experience, suddenly finding myself deserted by the park railings without so much as a farewell.

On the face of it, I should have been upset; after months of dedicated pursuit, unobtrusively putting myself in his way, annexing Jeff in the face of stiff competition, I'd undone the good work in 10 seconds flat. Maybe I was still too cross to care — yet.

NEXT day I kept probing my feelings cautiously, like a suspect tooth with an exploratory tongue. Still nothing — except a growing sense of release. Jeff, I realised, had taken a good deal of living up to.

As usual, Bay took me to Parkside that evening. I let him loose, and off he went, while I strolled idly after him, with a sense of having all the time in the world. There were one or two other dog walkers about, but no-one I knew.

Feeling vaguely disappointed, I left Bay longer than usual before calling him. He showed himself briefly in the distance, just to let me know his lack of co-operation was not entirely accidental. He approached in a leisurely, zig-zag fashion for some 10 yards, then was off again.

Smitted by what seemed a good idea, I pursed my lips and tried that special whistle. The trill wasn't so flute-like as *his* had been, last night, but it was a fair imitation. It fooled Bay, anyhow, who had probably thought I wasn't capable of doing it at all.

Over the grass he cantered expectantly — once again followed by that energetic ripple in his wake. At that point I had to admit to myself why I'd put on my new green jacket and biscuit trousers, instead of old duffel and jeans. My heart went bump as Bay stopped dead, and Blossom came hurtling at my legs making excited doggy noises, greeting an old friend.

Three more assorted dogs, also attracted by the whistle, lined up expectantly waiting for me to tell them what to do next. I could just imagine the tall, dark and handsome stranger's grin.

I glanced round quickly, but there was only a girl of about my own age hurrying towards me.

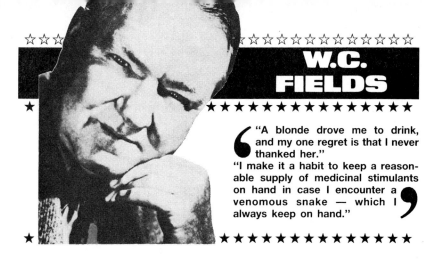

❛ "A blonde drove me to drink, and my one regret is that I never thanked her."
"I make it a habit to keep a reasonable supply of medicinal stimulants on hand in case I encounter a venomous snake — which I always keep on hand." ❜

★ ★★★★★★★★★★★★★★

She was small and slender, but otherwise the likeness was unmistakable. The amused dark eyes laughed at me as she captured the gambolling Blossom.

"Sorry, your whistle attracted her. She must have thought it was Tom."

"Tom?"

"My brother. I've had a broken ankle — only just out of plaster. He's been taking Blossom out for me."

Blossom adored me with bright eyes, totally forgiving me for any misjudgment.

"She's very friendly, isn't she?" I said, smiling.

The girl laughed. "So friendly that she's an embarrassment sometimes!"

She glanced at Bay, who was examining the distant horizon nonchalantly. He was obviously aware that if he took off again, it would be an admission that he'd been fooled.

"Tom was right — he's a magnificent dog."

Well — at least he'd a good opinion of *one* of us!

With a friendly goodnight, the girl ran off towards the road with Blossom. I took Bay home more soberly.

When I delivered him to Mrs Connington, she had a visitor. I'd seen him around the Conningtons' house before, a rather military-looking man with a neat grey moustache.

Bay recognised him, too, even going so far as to approach him and indicate that a pat would not go amiss.

"Jean — you remember Robert Sneddon — an old friend of my husband's?" Mrs Connington asked. "We've been having a long chat about Bay, and I've decided to let Robert take him. You've been so good, dear, but I don't think it's fair on you or Bay. He's always been a man's dog."

I was surprised at the pang I felt, and the empty feeling as I crossed the road to my parents' house. Silly! I scolded myself. How could I possibly miss that superior dog more than I missed Jeff?

NEXT evening I couldn't settle to doing any of the things I used to say I would, if it wasn't for Bay's demands on my time. It must be just the change in the established routine, I told myself irritably.

I went up to the library — but coming back to Parkside, I stopped resisting temptation, and turned in at the gate. After all, there was no law prohibiting unaccompanied dog walkers from enjoying the amenities.

I saw Tom in the distance before he saw me, and was seized by a sudden impulse to purse my lips and whistle. Alarmed at my impulse, I clamped my jaws firmly together — I didn't want him to think that I was an idiot, as well as rude and incapable.

When we came abreast, he stopped. His dark eyes scanned Parkside.

"Lost him again?"

"No. He's gone to live with a friend of the family. Someone he has a higher opinion of than me."

"You're missing him?"

"Strangely enough, yes!"

It was my turn to look around. "Your sister hasn't broken her other ankle, I hope?"

"No. She came here for a change last night, because I said Parkside was a good place for dogs. But she prefers to take Blossom nearer home. We live on the other side of town."

"So you're here for a walk, too?"

"Well, it is a nice night . . ."

He smiled at me, and it was somehow different from that impersonal friendly grin. There was warmth in his eyes, and a responsive leaping of my heart.

"I like you in green," he said. "It matches your eyes."

We began to walk. Our steps matched perfectly.

"Tell me," he said. "What kind of dogs do you like?"

"Something with character. Like Bay, only not so big. And you?"

"Oh — lovable types like Blossom, only not so small. Perhaps we could agree on something?"

"Oh, I'd think so!" I agreed impulsively. The blushing started again. "By the way," I added hastily, "I expect your sister told you — I found your whistle very successful. Though I didn't get the trill quite right."

"Show me," he invited.

I obliged.

"Ah — it's the flute bit. It goes up-down-up. Listen."

He demonstrated.

"Look!" I said, clutching his arm with sweet familiarity.

Assorted dogs were advancing from all directions, panting eagerly. We fled, slamming the park gates behind us just in time, and walked away laughing helplessly, hand-in-hand.

———————— * **THE END** * ————————

DAY OF SURPRISES

He'd been so busy arranging his daughter's wedding, he hadn't noticed she had plans of her own — for him!

Complete Story By
CHARLES C. O'CONNELL

PROMPTLY at four o'clock in the afternoon, Roy Garrett was joined by his daughter's bridesmaid. She came through the glass doors from the garden interrupting his restless pacing around the living-room.

He stared at her in disbelief, as though she were a stranger who had lost her way and had stumbled into his home by accident.

She wore a denim jacket and jeans, and tufts of her blonde, cropped hair stood up on the crown of her head. She carried a small case, and seemed to be puzzled by his expression.

"I'm Suzanne," she said, as if she thought he hadn't recognised her. "I'm the bridesmaid. Remember?"

"I know," Roy said. He brushed his fingers across his forehead, his eyes on the pink toenails peeping out of her sandals. Then he added, "You're not going to the church like that, are you?"

She laughed at him, obviously understanding his bewilderment for the first time. "Of course not! I've got my things in the case. I must say you look very smart, Mr Garrett," she added.

He was wearing a dark suit, and an unfamiliar bow tie. He felt stiff, awkward and uneasy for this, his daughter's wedding day. Or, to be precise, wedding afternoon.

Fashions change, he thought. For his own wedding he'd worn tails. But that was long ago. In an age he could understand . . .

Ann, his daughter, called from upstairs: "Is that you, Suzanne?" Her voice was eager, happy.

"I'm coming up!" Suzanne yelled, and scampered for the stairs.

Roy continued his wandering around the room. He realised that many people would consider the living-room somewhat cluttered. There were books everywhere. "We really should do something with those books," his wife, Liz, had said once. "The house is getting like a public library."

Roy smiled wryly as he remembered his wife's words. She had been a wonderful companion, but his books had always come between her and her ambitions for their home.

"You couldn't possibly have read all of them," she'd said.

"I have," he'd told her. "And I'll read them again. I'm very lucky; I have a wonderful wife and a thousand trusted friends!"

Liz had laughed at him. Not derisively — understandingly. He had got his priorities right. She never mentioned the books again. A professor of English needed a lot of books . . .

HE wandered over to the glass doors. The garden wasn't a riot of colour, but it was familiar, comfortable, like an old suit. When Liz was alive it was always in perfect order. The problem for him was time, and, perhaps, enthusiasm. He enjoyed the garden — but didn't care for gardening.

Then he noticed the yellow sports car beyond the gate at the end of the short driveway. Somebody was behind the wheel, waiting. Roy walked down to it, and a young man sat up in the driver's seat.

He was sandy haired, freckled, and dressed soberly in black. His white shirt looked too big for him, and he didn't appear to be very happy. He looked familiar, somehow — Roy felt that they had met before.

"Are you with Suzanne?" he asked.

"Yes." The young man's voice was resigned, as if he were admitting to an affliction.

"Don't I know you from somewhere?"

"I'm Bob. David's best man."

"Oh," Roy said. The car gleamed garishly in the sun.

"Great day for the wedding." Bob fingered his white collar in an embarrassed way, drawing it closer around his neck, as though aware it was too big.

"Yes," Roy agreed, feeling older than his 48 years. "Would you like a drink?"

"No, no." Bob reacted as if he had been offered poison. "I'll just wait here."

"Is Suzanne going to the church with you?" Roy asked.

"Yes."

"In this car?"

"Sure." Bob looked puzzled.

"I've got to get back in," Roy said with a sigh. "It's nearly time. Excuse me." He glanced at his watch but the time didn't register. He realised he was as uneasy as the young man.

R OY walked up the drive towards the house. On his own wedding day there had been black, sedate limousines, one with white ribbons from the bonnet to the roof; chauffeurs with white coats and shiny, peaked caps. Only now did Roy realise that he hadn't liked them.

But a yellow sports car! Now that was really a bit much . . .

There had been a hundred guests at his wedding. It hadn't been a pretty wedding. Taken collectively, the relatives and friends of the bride and 'groom had not made an impressive assortment of human beauty. The assembly merely proved that human form was of infinite variety.

You should meet friends one at a time, Roy had thought. Seen all at once, they were a bit daunting . . .

Later, at the reception, with the inhibitions gone, the whole affair became a disagreeable farce. Liz had been the only reality. Serene, beautiful in white her eyes linking her heart to his.

BETTER THAN RADAR

When we moved house we received a lot of helpful advice from the previous owners. The tip that amused me most was:

"Whatever you do don't oil the garden gate. It's invaluable.

"One squeak is the milk arriving, two squeaks is the postman, and a long slow creak is the woman next door coming round to borrow something."

When they finally left for the airport her mother had cried as if he were taking her daughter to a fate worse than death.

That was why Roy hadn't objected when his daughter had told him that hers was going to be a quiet wedding.

"Who do you think we should invite?" he'd asked her.

"Nobody," she'd said firmly. Then paradoxically, "Just you, and Suzanne — she's going to be bridesmaid — and David's best friend at university for best man. And David's mother, of course."

"Quite a manageable number," Roy had said absently.

Ann had laughed at him and put her arms around his neck. "Oh, dear, dopy Daddy! You've never objected to anything I do, have you? You've really spoiled me completely . . ."

That wasn't true, Roy knew. Ann had grown gracious and beautiful all by herself.

"Why should I object?" he'd said. "You're your own property, love. You don't owe me a thing."

He'd been tempted to say how much he wished that her mother was alive to see her married. But he didn't. Ann didn't like sentiment, and besides, Liz was just a legend to Ann. She'd been only three years old when her mother died . . .

"You must take care of yourself," Liz had told him, fully aware of what was happening to herself. "You're a bit of a dreamer, you know — not quite aware of life." Then she'd smiled at him and squeezed his hand. "But I forgot your thousand trusted friends."

In his anguish Roy had said nothing. His books had been his only friends since she died. He'd known her just five years . . .

Roy realised he was becoming morose. He looked at his watch and the time took him by surprise. They'd better hurry!

He went to the foot of the stairs. "It's four-thirty!" he called up to his daughter.

"Be with you in a minute, Dad." Offhandedly, with no sense of urgency. As if time meant nothing, and the minister could wait indefinitely in the church on the hill . . .

"It seems a rather odd time of the day to be married," Roy had said to Ann. His own wedding had been on a bleak September day at ten o'clock in the morning. He'd been petrified with fear and cold, and he'd been worried about Liz in her flimsy white lace . . .

"Five o'clock is as good a time as any," Ann had told him. "People should feel free to marry at any time. I think five o'clock is a very practical time. We can have dinner instead of breakfast-cum-lunches. Don't worry, Dad. Five o'clock is the 'in' time now."

Roy had accepted that. Just like he'd accepted the church in which the ceremony was to take place. Ann and David had selected it because it was old, picturesque, and was on a hill.

But it was five miles away. To be there by five o'clock meant leaving right now, at this very moment, and driving at an average speed of 80 miles an hour, which was beyond the capabilities of his six-year-old car . . .

He went to the foot of the stairs to call up again but there was no need to say anything. Ann was coming down.

She wore a long floral dress with a high, ruffled neckline. She looked beautiful. Her resemblance to her mother was startling, and Roy was suddenly sorry that there wouldn't be a hundred guests.

Coming down behind his daughter, Suzanne appeared to have worked a miracle of transformation on herself. She wore a similar outfit to his daughter, but in a different floral pattern. Her short hair had been brushed into a semblance of order.

Ann had smiled at his open admiration of her. "All set, Dad?"

ANN came with him, while Suzanne went in the yellow sports car. Bob waited as though uncertain that Roy's old car would start, and then led the way out of the college grounds. Roy was grateful for that, since he had only a sketchy idea of the location of the church.

At the college gates some students had gathered, and they stormed hysterically around the two cars, slowing them to a crawl, and showering them with confetti and rice.

Everything seems in reverse nowadays, Roy thought. Rice and confetti came at the *end* of the ceremony, surely.

Beside him, Ann was laughing and waving, while ahead, Suzanne was shouting joyfully.

T HE small church was clean and bright, and empty except for two people who sat in one of the front pews. Suzanne and Bob hurried up towards the altar and sat down.

From the back of the church, where he stood with Ann, Roy saw a door open fractionally. Then Suzanne made a signal and the door opened wider. A young minister came out on to the altar. From somewhere an organ pumped out Mendelssohn's "Wedding March."

"OK, Dad," Ann whispered, squeezing Roy's arm.

They walked slowly up to the aisle. The minister who waited for them, smilingly, was little more than a boy himself. Roy saw David glance back once, and then he left his seat to stand at the altar rails.

The short, simple ceremony was moving and beautiful. Roy was astonished to see how dignified these young people looked and behaved. Yet there was an atmosphere of lightness around the altar.

His own ceremony had been a very serious business. The minister has been old, and a trifle absent minded, as if this particular duty had interrupted something more important. Roy remembered his own sense of incredulity when the ceremony was over. Was he actually married . . . ? Liz had never had any doubts.

He glanced across the aisle and intercepted the eyes of David's mother — fleetingly, since she turned her gaze away immediately.

He wondered what she was thinking about. He guessed that she would probably be as lonely as he would himself after his daughter was gone. Ann had told him her future mother-in-law had been a widow for more than 10 years.

Roy had seen her just once before. It was customary for the mother of the 'groom to see the father of the bride at least once before the marriage. They had met at his house, which stood on the perimeter of the college grounds. It had been a quiet, polite meeting. David and Ann had played host and hostess, mainly to themselves.

David's mother was a very lovely, competent, artistic woman. She designed exclusive clothes, and had managed for herself and her only son very capably indeed since her husband's death. She radiated independence. Inevitably she had commented on his books . . .

"You seem to have a lot of them."

"Yes," he'd replied. "But I find them all very interesting."

He found she was looking at him intently — but with a gentle, sympathetic expression.

"You'll miss Ann very much," she'd said.

"Yes," he'd replied. "Of course. But no more than you will, David."

Her eyes had remained on him as if she'd discovered something on his face of which he was completely unaware.

Continued on page 130

A Real Sew-And-Sew — That's Me!

It's no wonder I get needled sometimes, says Lisa Stewart, when people keep buttonholing me with impossible requests . . .

IF you've ever thought of saving yourself some money by making your own clothes — beware.

I'll guarantee that, because of it, you'll acquire a host of distant relatives you didn't know you had.

And neighbours who barely had a passing nod to spare before, will suddenly decide they don't see nearly enough of you.

That's certainly what happened to me after I went to dressmaking classes at night school.

Now, a mysterious grapevine seemed to operate the minute a home dressmaker takes the cover off her newly-bought sewing machine.

Soon, everyone knows about it.

First there's a hint that: "Clothes are so expensive these days."

That's followed by the wistful: "If only I knew a good dressmaker . . ."

And before you know it, you've a stack of orders longer than your tape measure.

"There's no hurry, dear," you'll be told. "But the dance is on Friday — and I haven't a thing to wear."

If I had a pound for every time I'd heard that . . .

Surprisingly enough, it was that very thought — money — which first prompted me to think about setting up in business.

After all, I thought, I'd been making clothes for myself and other people for years.

I hadn't a single complaint — but I hadn't received a single penny either!

So I decided to stop being an unpaid servant and put things on a proper business footing.

If you're thinking of doing the same thing, perhaps I can help you avoid some of the pitfalls I fell into.

Setting up your own dressmaking business shouldn't require too much investment.

After all, most amateur dressmakers already have the biggest essential item — a sewing machine.

In fact, that — plus a small advert in your local paper or shop — is all you really need to start.

MY advert brought an almost overwhelming response — it seems there's a great demand for dressmakers these days.

I could see myself rivalling Mary Quant in no time.

My first problem was over what to charge.

I still blush when I recall the embarrassing "What do I owe you?" "Well, what do you think it's worth?" session with my first paying client.

Not very professional.

After that, I did what I should have done at the start — and

drew up a scale of charges.

I decided that, taking everything into account, I should charge £3 an hour.

After the first few weeks I had to revise that.

I found I was inundated with the dressmakers' nightmare — alterations.

"Just a little tuck in there," or "Could you give me another inch over the hips?"

Not only are alterations very time consuming, they're boring.

Even what seems a minor change can involve unpicking large areas and re-sewing them.

I upped my alteration charge to £4 per hour and, although there's been no drop in demand, I earn a bit more for doing it.

A word of warning — always measure each client before each order and always measure them yourself.

Your tape measure may not lie, but theirs certainly does!

The years have a way of creeping up behind a woman and drastically altering the dress size she fondly remembers she had.

I also have clients who can change as much as two dress sizes from autumn to spring.

A HAIRDRESSER friend once told me her least-favourite clients were the ones who came in with a picture of a glamorous film star and asked to look like the star.

I have the same problem.

Why do nice, plump, matronly ladies insist on bringing me patterns that need a figure like Twiggy's ?

Ladies who are "large made" insist on buying material with massive checks which, from the rear, make them look like a section of girders on the Forth Bridge.

I try to tactfully suggest they reconsider, but they rarely do, so the finished product isn't exactly the kind of advertisement for my work I want.

It's now several years since I "turned professional," and I've never regretted it.

Orders come in steadily, and from what I earn I'm able to make my own clothes with no drain on the housekeeping.

But don't expect to make your fortune. I'm still waiting for the diamond jewellery! ■

Continued from page 127

"I'll miss David," she'd said. "But I work, you see. It won't be as if I were at home all the time waiting for him to come in."

"I'm glad," he'd told her. "As for myself — I teach, as you probably know. So I've got quite a few other children."

She'd smiled at him then, as though she'd found something very satisfactory in what he'd said.

"We're both lucky, then Mr Garrett."

This afternoon she was dressed in blue. It gave Roy a sense of pleasure that she wasn't wearing a hat — the hats at his own wedding had been terrible. David's mother wore a veil of embroidered lace over her fair hair . . .

THE six of them had dinner in the Park Hotel. A special room had been reserved for them, overlooking the city. It was almost dark and the lights below glittered like stars.

Roy sat beside David's mother. She was watching the four young people chattering and laughing around a stereo set in a corner.

Roy thought she looked worried. He wanted to tell her what a wonderful person Ann was. Parents reassured in-laws like that.

Instead he said, "I think they'll be very happy."

She looked at him in surprise. "Why, of course. They're in love with each other."

Of course. He felt like a fool. He should have known that nothing else mattered except their feelings for one another.

"It was a nice ceremony," he said.

"It was," she agreed.

"Different to my own," he went on.

"Mine, too."

Roy paused for a moment, uncertain as to what to say next. "I think it's better this way," he said finally.

David's mother looked puzzled. "What way?"

"I mean, a quiet wedding."

The stereo was playing a pop tune loudly.

She looked at him gravely. "I think so," she said.

The dinner was a great success. The pattern and depth of the young people's conversation surprised Roy. Beneath everything they said was a feeling for each other and humanity in general.

There was concern without hoplessness, and beneath the banter, a quiet confidence concerning their own studies. David had one more year to go before his engineering degree, while Ann was battling her way towards her B.A. in modern languages.

Once again Roy felt David's mother watching him, and this time she didn't glance away when he looked at her. They smiled at each other understandingly. This generation was different to their own, but each generation was linked together, and they were still involved in the changing life around them.

It was almost midnight when it came to an end. David and Ann were leaving for a secret honeymoon. Suzanne and Bob were going to their respective homes.

Ann wanted a private word with Roy while David was saying

goodbye to his mother. She gave him a small packet. He looked at it blankly. He hadn't expected anything . . .

"What is it?" he asked.

"There are two spark plugs in that," Ann told him. "David took them out of his mother's car."

Roy looked at her in alarm. "Why did he do that?"

"Because when his mother can't start the car, you'll have to drive her home. You'd never have thought of that yourself."

"I certainly wouldn't take the plugs out of her car . . ."

"She's lovely, Dad," Ann said. "Books aren't so hot as full-time companions really."

She kissed him on the cheek.

"Goodbye for a while, Dad. Think it over."

Roy returned to the dining-room to find it empty except for David's mother. He felt unhappy and conspiratorial when he saw her glance at the small package he held in his hand.

"You'll find you won't be able to start your car," he said.

"Oh." She looked at him without surprise.

He unwrapped the package and showed her the plugs. "David and Ann removed these from your car."

"Why should they do a thing like that?"

Roy felt embarrassed. "So that I would have to drive you home. I . . . I felt I had to tell you, although it spoils their plans for us."

She looked from the plugs to his face. "It would be rather tedious putting them back in the dark," she said.

"I don't think I know how."

"Then you won't mind dropping me off in your car?"

"Of course not."

As he started the car outside the hotel, he said, "You'll think me very stupid, but the fact is I don't remember your first name."

"It's Clare."

"Mine is —"

"Oh, I know yours," she said.

He smiled at her in the darkness of the car, feeling an unaccountable sense of pleasure that she knew his christian name . . .

———————— * **THE END** * ————————

Beth was gone — yet she was the onl

K IM was so like Beth that she took Jean Raeburn's breath away.
For one dizzy moment she thought that Beth had been given
back to her.

But it was three years, three long years of sorrow, since Beth had
died . . .

Then Kim had been four, soft and chubby, her features still
forming. But now, as Jean gazed at her granddaughter, the dark
eyes and hair, the grave little mouth, were a perfect replica. A
miniature Beth.

"Hello, Kim," she said unsteadily. "Did you enjoy the ride on the
aeroplane?"

"Yes, thank you, Granny." The little girl was composed. Beth had

Complete Story By ISOBEL STEWART

LOVE IS ALL

ne who could bring them together . . .

been the same, all her joy and sorrow had been hidden behind a serious face.

Jean wasn't sure how to go on. Kim, after all, was a stranger. And all because Stephen, lost and bewildered by Beth's death, had taken the child and himself to live with his mother.

Jean and her husband, David, had often planned the long trip to visit Kim and Stephen, but every time the moment approached, something happened.

Now, with what seemed bewildering speed, Kim had come to them.

It had all been in the letter from Stephen. He was going to marry Jenny, the girl who lived next door. And as his mother was going into hospital soon afterwards, could they possible care for Kim for a

133

few weeks until he and Jenny came for her?

Could they!

Jean had cried that night for the first time in months. She cried for the little granddaughter she didn't know, for herself and for David. But, most of all, she cried for Beth, who had died so young, and her new baby with her.

In her misery, Jean lay in the darkness hoping the tears would soften her grief.

"Why didn't you wake me, love?" David asked in the morning, when he saw her tear-torn face and knew that she had passed the previous night without sleep.

"Jean, three years is a long time. Stephen's young. This Jenny will be good for him, and good for Kim, too."

She knew all that; her head accepted it — it was only her heart that couldn't. Somehow it seemed as if Stephen was going to put somebody in Beth's place . . .

Of course, she longed to see her granddaughter, but it was a mixed longing. For three years she had been wrapping protective layers around her grief. She'd almost convinced herself it was healed but now Kim's coming had pierced the shield. And suddenly the wound was as raw as ever.

KIM was waiting patiently. Jean shook herself. "Would you like some ice-cream? It's a long drive home."

"I had ice-cream on the plane, thank you. Daddy and Jenny told the air hostess I liked it."

"Oh." She picked up Kim's case and walked her to the car. "Was it a nice wedding?" she asked steadily.

"It was lovely. Jenny wore a hat of flowers and I had flowers to carry. We had tiny sausage rolls, and cheese on sticks."

"It sounds lovely," Jean said.

Kim sat upright on the seat next to Jean, looking straight ahead at the road. Jean looked swiftly at the serious face and wondered helplessly if she was unhappy.

After all, her father had married again, there was a new mother, a visit to a forgotten grandmother . . . It was a lot for a little girl to take.

She knew that Beth would have resented all the changes and her unhappiness would have shown itself in something tangible.

Was Kim the same? Was she, secretly, in turmoil? Or was she simply the well-mannered, composed little girl she appeared to be?

By the time they'd reached home David was already there. He was raking the lawn and Jean knew he was trying not to look as if he was waiting.

"There's your grandfather," she told Kim.

"I remember him!" There was surprise in Kim's face and voice. "I know your face, too. Not just from photographs, but really."

"It was a long time ago." Jean leant over to open the door so Kim could get out.

"Hello, Kim, why don't you come and see my fish," David said warmly, holding out his hand. Kim hesitated, then she smiled and put her hand in his.

Jean's hurt eased a little. The child knew and accepted her grandfather. As she walked behind them to the house and saw her big husband bend to listen to something Kim was saying, she knew that they would get on. The signs of friendship were already showing . . .

David switched on the light behind the fish tank and Kim drew in her breath with wonder.

"Would you like to feed them?" David offered and Kim nodded seriously, her eyes on the darting little fish.

David measured the food and, solemnly, Kim sprinkled it on the water. Involuntarily, Jean's eyes met David's; and she knew that they were both seeing another little girl doing the same thing a long time ago.

"Would you like to see your room now?" asked Jean after the fish had been fed.

IT had been Beth's room and even now it was still the same. Waiting, Jean often felt helplessly, for her to come back.

She always kept telling herself to change it, perhaps into a sewing-room. *Telling* herself; never doing it.

As she opened the door for Kim, she was glad everything was still the same — right down to the rose-sprigged curtains.

"Do you like it?" she asked Kim tentatively, but then she stopped. "Sooty!" she exclaimed sternly.

The big black cat was asleep on the bedspread. He opened his eyes and looked at her. Then, deliberately, he turned his back and went to sleep again.

Jean laughed. It was so typical of Sooty.

Kim bubbled with excitement. "Is it really Sooty? Granny, is it Sooty? My mummy's Sooty?"

"Do you remember Sooty?" asked Jean. But the words she couldn't say were there as well: *Do you remember her, Beth? Your mother, my daughter?*

Kim nodded and smiled the wide, gap-toothed smile of a happy seven-year-old.

"Sooty did it the other time, too," Kim went on eagerly. "I came in the car with Mummy and Daddy and when we got out you were here and Grandad was here. Mummy kissed you and she kissed Grandad and everybody was talking.

"I wanted my dolly and Mummy said it was in the suitcase so we all came here. And Sooty was sleeping, just like that. Mummy spoke to him and he purred and purred."

Jean's eyes filled with tears.

"Do you remember, Granny? I'm right, aren't I?"

Jean nodded and blinked, remembering every minute of that last visit.

She could still see Beth sitting on the bed, her dark hair hiding her face which lay against the cat's gleaming fur. And her voice, soft with wonder as the cat purred and rubbed against her.

"Nearly a year, Mum," she'd said in wonderment, "and he still remembers!"

After Beth had gone, Jean often wondered if Sooty, his head on one side, was waiting for footsteps that never came.

AFTER Kim's arrival it seemed the old cat's waiting was over. For a long time he had eaten and slept, purring only when Jean stroked him. An old, tired cat dreaming his way to the end of his days.

But with Kim he regained youth — or tried to. He followed her round the house, dignified and slow. When he paused, he looked about as if interested in something, when really he was finding enough breath to go on.

David had given Kim fish of her own to keep, ordinary goldfish that swum around in an old fish-bowl. And every day when she fed them the old black cat would watch and wait patiently for her to come back to him.

Kim was a quiet child but often, as she played with the cat, she would give a gurgle or laughter. It was something of her own that had nothing of Beth in it.

Once, when she laughed, Jean instinctively hugged her and there was no withdrawal, no shrinking back. Instead, the warm little arms clung round her neck and Jean knew Kim had accepted her, too.

And once that total acceptance was there, Kim became curious.

She asked about her mother. And, with a confusing blend of joy and sorrow, Jean answered her questions, her memory producing little incidents, polished and cherished with love, which she gave to the child like small gifts.

Kim asked about Sooty and all the other cats and dogs they'd had. Jean told her as best she could, not always clear in her own mind which adventure happened to this cat or that. The years of her children's young days ran together in a confusion of happiness.

"Was Sooty the fighter?" asked Kim one day.

Jean looked at the old cat asleep in the sun and smiled. "Oh, he was the greatest fighter we ever had. Your mother was always having to nurse his wounds."

"Tell me." Jean loved the command in the little voice.

"Well, he disappeared once for a whole week. Your mummy was so worried, then your Uncle Peter found him lying under that lilac bush over there. He was covered in dirt and his leg was hurt so badly that he couldn't move."

"And his ears?" Kim prompted.

"And his ears," Jean agreed. "Uncle Peter said Sooty was dead. Mummy was doing her homework but she jumped up and said he *mustn't* be dead."

Jean closed her eyes and leant against the warm stone of the old

136

house. She saw the slight figure and the fierce eyes dark in a white face and the cat lying in the thin arms. And the determined voice saying, "I won't let him die, Mummy. He can't die."

Only her dark eyes showed her grief and, later, her gentleness as she bathed the wounds.

"And he didn't die, did he?" chimed in Kim anxiously. She wouldn't believe the arrogant warrior of long ago was the same cat slumbering at her feet.

"No, he didn't die," Jean assured her. "He lived to tell the tale."

Kim giggled as she always did when Jean said that.

SLOWLY, sweetly, Jean and David and Kim grew close. It was a quieter, softer closeness than that shared with even Beth, for 20 years ago their lives had been so different.

Then, Jean's life had been full and busy, always coming and going, with precious little time to sit in the sunshine with a child. But now she had the time and she found that to be quiet together was nice.

When David came home in the evenings, his eyes would be on the small, waiting figure swinging on the garden gate.

And at night, long after Kim was asleep, Jean and David would sit together. And they would smile, both of them thinking of her.

One night a mist came in from the sea making the air cold enough for a fire, and so they made one. And Kim sat in front of it, the glow reflecting on her face and pink dressing-gown.

"Do you always have a fire when it's cold?" she asked.

"Yes," said David. "It seems friendly somehow."

"My other gran had a fireplace but she said it made everything dirty so we had a switch-on heater." Kim thought about it and looked at the leaping flames. "It was warm but it didn't look so nice."

Jean's eyes filled with tears as she realised that there was a whole chunk of Kim's life that she didn't know about.

She remembered the nights when Beth and Peter sat in front of the fire, just like Kim now, pink and scrubbed for bed.

SISTERLY LOVE?

My sister got married recently, but before she did everyone assured me I'd miss her when she left home. How right they were!

I can't pinch her tights when mine are in tatters; there's nobody to argue with about the washing-up and, worst of all, I've got to buy my own make-up now.

Yes, there's certainly been an empty space in my purse since she got married.

Her memory produced more images: Beth, a long-legged schoolgirl stretched out on the rug; a teenager painstakingly painting her toenails while Peter teased . . .

And then there was the finest memory of all, sitting by the fire in the quiet evening, smiling sleepily at the glowing embers, a new baby in her arms — Kim.

Continued on page 140

A Cry In The Night...

SEVERAL years ago, when I had just left training college after qualifying as a teacher, I was sent to a small town school.

When I arrived, the headmaster advised me to see a certain lady about lodgings. I had never been in this town prior to that day, and I knew no-one at all.

At the end of my interview at the school, I made my way to the lady's house, as the headmaster had suggested.

When I explained to her why I was there, she surprised me by asking where I lived — and when I told her the name of the village, she said, "I was expecting you. Last night I looked over a map of England and saw that name, and knew I'd have a caller from there."

On the strength of this, she offered to take me as a paying guest.

Many times while I lived with her, I experienced her uncanny association with the supernatural, and her accurate forecasting of future events.

But there was one event in particular which above all others convinced me that this lady could see things which were hidden from ordinary eyes.

Very early one morning, at a quarter to three precisely, I was suddenly awakened from a deep sleep by my landlady, who was fully dressed, and carrying a handbag.

Wondering what on earth was the matter, I sat up quickly and asked her what was going on.

To my utter amazement she calmly said, "I have to go to Guildford in Surrey at once — my son has just had an accident."

Naturally, I thought she had been dreaming, as it was so early in the morning. Obviously there was no post at that time, and we were not on the telephone. How could she possibly have found out about such an accident?

When she saw that I was doubtful she repeated her story, and added several details to it. She told me that her son had been to a dance and had left the hall at two in the morning to cycle home to his aunt's house, where he was living.

A few minutes later he had been thrown from his bicycle and knocked unconscious on the road.

At the time of falling she had clearly heard him cry out: "Mother!"

My landlady then said he had knocked out his two front teeth and cut his chin, besides being bruised.

can you explain it?

Having given me all these details, which she said she'd seen quite clearly, she then informed me that she was going to catch the next train to Guildford, due in half an hour from the local station, to see her son.

Then she asked me to look after myself until her return.

I was very sceptical about the whole affair. I'd never had any experience of things like this — so I just didn't believe them.

A DAY or two later a letter came from my landlady. In it she said that her "vision" had been correct in practically every detail!

She said that when she arrived on the doorstep of her brother's house in Guildford, her sister-in-law nearly fainted at the sight of her there so early in the morning, and without having heard any word from her about the accident.

My landlady said that her son was in bed, badly bruised, with a deep cut on his chin, and his two front teeth were broken, although not actually knocked out.

Her son confirmed that he did call out "Mother" as he fell.

A few weeks later my landlady's son came home for a short holiday, and I was able to see for myself the deep scar on his chin and the broken front teeth.

It was incredible — but how could I doubt any longer that my landlady had powers beyond those of normal people . . . ? ∎

It was a cry of despair, in a lonely country lane, miles from anywhere. But, says Mrs M. Lankups, it still reached out to the person it was meant for . . .

Continued from page 137

LATER that night, when Kim was asleep, Jean brought the tea-tray to the fire.

"We'll show Kim how to make toast tomorrow," David said. "That ought to be useful in winter."

"In winter," Jean said quietly, "Kim won't be here." Then she told him about the thought growing slowly in her mind, becoming a part of her.

"David. Couldn't we ask Stephen if we could keep her?" She saw his eyes and rushed on. "She's so happy here. With us, the cat and her fish.

"Stephen and this Jenny — surely it would be better for them to start on their own. They'll have their own family and — and then Kim will be the odd one out."

David put down his pipe. "You're seeing things the way you want to see them, love. Stephen is Kim's father. How can you ask him to give her up?"

She shook her head in defiance; as the idea had taken hold, she had convinced herself David would agree.

He sat on the arm of her chair and drew her head against him. She resisted, stiff and bitterly disappointed.

"Jean, listen," he said firmly. "Kim is all Stephen has left of Beth."

"But he's married again!"

"Yes, but that doesn't change the fact he loved Beth. And Kim is their daughter — his as well as hers."

Jean stayed silent and he tried again. "If you had died when Beth and Peter were small, do you think I would have let them go?"

"But that's different," she whispered.

"No, it isn't, love." His gentleness unnerved her and she began to cry. "Jean, the best thing for Kim is her own father, a nice new mother and some brothers and sisters. She needs all that. She's a lonely child, you know."

Jean looked at him with surprise. "She's perfectly happy. She has us, the cat and — and her fish."

He looked at her steadily and said nothing. She felt warm colour tinge her cheeks and without another word she carried the tea-tray to the kitchen.

David followed and, after a moment, she turned to him. She stayed in his arms, not crying, but soaking up comfort from his closeness.

THE next day a letter came from Peter and Lucy telling them they could expect a new grandchild. Peter reminded them of their promise to visit, and asked if they could time it for when the baby came.

Lucy, wrote Peter, says she has no idea how to handle a baby and would be happy if you could be here to help.

"I could arrange things," said David. "Lucy has nobody of her own, after all. Tell them we'll come, love. You'd like that, wouldn't you?"

Not Very Adult, I Fear!

WHY . . . why . . . why do I do it? I'm a fairly stable, reasonably sensible adult. Why then, when I walk into a dentist's surgery — or even his waiting-room — do I immediately begin to act like a gibbering, nervous eight-year-old?

Someone please tell me, because I've just done it again this morning — after telling myself not to be silly.

Yet silly I was. And I can't blame my dentist, or his charming assistant. They greeted me like a long-lost friend.

How was I, he asked as he washed his hands. And wasn't it a lovely day?

My scintillating reply? "Y-yes. Fine. Fine!"

Then I proceeded to trip going towards the chair, and lean on the swivel tray that held his instruments. Needless to say, it swivelled!

At last I sat in the sumptuously upholstered chair, there was a humming sound and slowly the chair tilted back. Immediately my heart-rate doubled.

As he began his explorations I closed my eyes and tried again to reason out my ridiculous behaviour.

Perhaps it goes back to my childhood. I can still remember those regular checks we had at school.

They always seemed to come on a day when all was right with my world. The mere sight of those white coats and those pink cards with rows of teeth on them sent my spirits sinking.

Suddenly the humming began again. The chair was straightening, my bib was being removed.

What was he saying? My teeth were fine? Before I knew it I was outside blinking in the sunshine.

As I made my way to the office I wanted to sing. But, then, that would have been just as ridiculous.

Jean said she would, and after the letter was written she went upstairs. She took out the cherished christening robe both Beth and Peter had worn. This new baby was far less real to her than Kim, who had worn it last.

"Did Daddy send it back after Mummy died?" asked Kim. "I remember we did take it back home with us that time, didn't we? Her voice became uncertain. "For the baby that died when Mummy died?"

Jean flinched at the child's directness. "Yes, Daddy sent it back."

Kim touched the embroidered robe. "I wish that baby hadn't died. If God wanted Mummy he might have left the baby for me."

And it was then that Jean realised the thing that had bothered her. And it had taken the child to show her that grandparents, an old cat, and fish were not enough — that Kim needed, and *wanted*, so much more.

And from then on Jean accepted that when the time came, Kim would have to go.

Kim liked to talk about Jenny. Jean could see she was ready to love her. She told herself this was wonderful. She wouldn't have to worry about Kim.

Yet a small nagging ache remained; this Jenny had not only taken Beth's place with Stephen, she had taken Beth's place with the child.

TWO days before Stephen and Jenny came for Kim, the old cat's second spring was over. Sooty simply fell asleep in his favourite place in the sun and didn't wake up.

David told Jean and they both went to Kim. She didn't cry, just insisted David bury the cat under the lilac bush.

But that night she lay silently in bed with her face turned to the wall. Just how Beth would have reacted, Jean thought.

"Kim, darling," she said, "we'll see Mrs Easton along the road tomorrow. Her cat's had kittens. If there is a black one like Sooty you shall have it."

Kim looked at the empty space at the bottom of the bed where Sooty had loved to curl up, and shook her head. "No, I don't want one like Sooty. There will only be one Sooty and he's dead."

She cried and Jean held her close, relieved that, finally, tears had come. When Kim finally fell asleep the stony look was gone from her small face.

The next day she was quiet, but the worst of her grieving was done. "He was very old, Granny. I suppose he thought he had lived long enough."

Stephen phoned in the evening, and after settling his anxious questions about Kim, Jean told him about the cat.

"Poor old Sooty," said Stephen. "Do you remember how pleased Beth always was when he remembered her?"

I remember, Jean thought, as she replaced the reciver, but I didn't think you would, Stephen, not now you've married your Jenny . . .

JEAN was glad it was Saturday and David was home while she packed Kim's luggage. It hurt to see the rose-sprigged room look so empty again.

"What about my fish, Grandad?" Kim asked anxiously.

"I'll look after them," replied David easily. "Then every time you come on holiday you can see how they're doing."

Kim looked doubtful. "Couldn't I take them with me?"

"You could, but then Granny and I won't be able to look at your fish bowls and say, 'Of course Kim will be back soon. She has to come to see her fish.'"

Kim giggled for the first time since the cat died.

"Silly. I'll come to see you and Granny, anyway. I'll come often. Often!" Her face wrinkled for a moment. "Maybe I will leave them. Then when I'm lonely for you I can tell Daddy and Jenny it's time I saw how my fish are doing."

Long before it was time for Stephen to arrive, Kim was at the gate. Jean, busy in the kitchen, knew again David had been right. There was no room for doubt where Kim belonged when the car pulled up. The restless, waiting figure flew into her father's arms and then into Jenny's.

When Jenny put Kim down and straightened, Jean could see her properly. Fair hair, ruffled by Kim's hug, clear blue eyes in a suntanned face.

She isn't anything like Beth, Jean thought with amazement. She's quite, quite, different . . .

"Hello," said Jenny shyly. "It's nice to meet you at last, lovely to see Kim so well."

"Won't you come in?" Jean asked a little stiffly. "Lunch is almost ready."

Jenny lifted a wicker basket out of the car. Jean, remembering Kim's passionate voice, felt her heart sink. If they'd brought another Sooty . . .

"A present," said Jenny to Kim, "from me and Daddy."

Kim opened the basket and Jean saw two golden heads with floppy ears looking out. Puppies!

"Two?" questioned Kim, stroking the silky heads.

JUST A PHASE . . .

I seem to have missed the stage in my life when I was "up to date." Why?

Well, as a teenager "I thought I knew it all." But as a young wife "I had much to learn."

And when I became the mother of teenagers, "I was a bit of a square."

Now I'm a granny and "past it"!

[But we think you're very "with it."]

"One for you — for us," Jenny corrected quickly, "and one for Grandad and Granny." She looked at Jean. "I hope you don't mind. It seemed the best way to thank you for looking after Kim."

Jean felt the girl meant a lot more than she actually said. "Of course I don't mind," she replied. "I'm pleased," and she also meant much more than she said.

Jenny followed Jean into the kitchen.

"I'm glad you didn't get another kitten," Jean said.

Jenny's eyes widened. "I knew Kim wouldn't want that — she wouldn't want anything to take the cat's place. But the puppy's new, different. He'll be able to make a place of his own."

Jean's hands, busy serving lunch, stilled. The truth was as simple as that; this girl wasn't taking Beth's place, she was making a place of her own.

Something eased inside Jean. It might not be the last of the grief melting away, but it was most of it. Her hands grew busy again, and she smiled as she talked to Jenny about Kim.

And she knew that, if Jenny asked, she would even be able to talk about Beth.

─────────── * **THE END** * ───────────

JUST

"GET RID OF IT," HER FAMILY TOLD HER, FORGETTING IT WAS HER ONLY LINK WITH THE LITTLE GIRL WHO'D ONCE PLAYED IT.

**Complete Story
By
ELIZABETH FARRANT**

B UT, Mum — there just won't be room for it!" Lorna protested. "Not in a tiny flat."

"Just think — you'll be cluttered even as it is," Eileen urged. "Those heavy chairs, and that enormous sideboard . . ."

"I can't think what you want with a piano," Frances said, with just the smallest hint of irritation. "I mean, it's not as if it's ever *played!*"

Rose Prescott looked helplessly at her three daughters and sighed — a gentle sigh, half of appeal and half of resignation.

The girls — she still thought of them as girls, though Frances, her youngest, had two children of her own and Lorna, the eldest, had a teenage son — meant well, she knew.

Rose couldn't think how she'd have coped without them — particularly in those last six months when she'd been newly widowed and alone.

All through her married life it had been John who had made the big decisions for her. Now, in the bleak bewilderment after his death, she found herself leaning more and more upon her married daughters.

And of course they'd been wonderful, all three of them. Always at hand, ready and willing to give advice and help.

It had been Lorna who had first persuaded Rose that the old family house was far too big for one.

It had been Eileen's husband who had miraculously found Rose a flat — modern, incredibly compact and "just the thing."

Frances had solved the decorating problems. She'd decided on pale walls, white doors, white ceiling — "to give a sense of space."

And no unnecessary furniture. On that they were all agreed.

144

AN OLD PIANO

But when you were old, Rose thought, it wasn't space you wanted. It was a sense of — well, familiarity. A feeling of belonging . . .

That "clutter" which the girls despised so much could tell the whole story of your married life. Something unchanging, something you could cling to in a bewilderingly changing world.

The girls were still young, of course. They didn't understand . . .

Rose had been lost in thought. She roused herself reproachfully, aware of a sudden bustle of departure.

" 'Bye, Mum. Take care."

They each kissed Rose in turn. "And, Mum, *do* think again about that old piano."

Rose nodded and smiled a little ruefully. For the past few days she'd thought of little else.

A LONE in her comfortable, slightly shabby sitting-room, she gazed at the clumsy old instrument and touched it gently — its sleek, well-polished lid, its yellowing keys. Frances' words came back to her: *I mean . . . it's not as if it's ever played . . .*

No, it was never played these days, Rose thought. It had not been played, in fact, for years — not since the girls were small.

All three had taken lessons in their turn — Lorna, Eileen and Frances. First with indifference and later under protest. Finally Rose had faced the inevitable truth — none of them had the slightest ear for music.

The truth had been hard to face — because of Janey.

Delving a little deeper into her memories, Rose re-discovered her as she so often did. That first small daughter who had learned to sing almost as quickly as she'd learned to talk.

Janey had found magic in the sound of music.

She heard herself and John, two proud young parents, discussing what had then been a major problem . . .

"A piano!" Rose had gasped. "Can we afford it?"

Continued overleaf

"Of course we can't," he'd told her. "But we must. Janey's our only one — and she deserves her chance."

The piano they had chosen with such care was delivered one sunny morning, arriving in time for Janey's seventh birthday. Received with cries of awe and admiration, installed with ceremony, given pride of place.

And Janey had more than justified its purchase. Right from that memorable first music lesson, she'd shown a most amazing aptitude.

Practice had been a joy, never a burden. Her small slim fingers rippled up and down the keyboard; her gentle touch made the piano sing.

Rose had paused often in her household chores — she'd worked so quickly, anyway, in those days — to listen to those first short, simple pieces. There was one which had always been her favourite — "A Dream In Springtime." She still kept the music sheet.

She'd been so proud the day Miss Marlowe, Janey's music teacher, had told her earnestly, "That child of yours is gifted, Mrs Prescott. Just wait a few years, and she'll really surprise you both. She should go far one day . . ."

Miss Marlowe was not to know — no-one could know — that Janey, her small star pupil, so young, so bright, so much in love with life, had only one year left for making music, and less than two to live.

Rose sighed, remembering . . .

Now Janey seemed so far — so far away that it was sometimes hard to reach her, even in dreams. But somehow the piano brought her closer . . .

It would be hard, Rose thought, to part with it. But of course the girls were right. The flat was *very* small . . .

NEXT day the three of them called in as usual. "Oh, while I remember, Mum," Lorna said briskly, when they had settled down to a spot of tea, "I've made some enquiries for you — about the piano. It seems you just have to phone the District Council and they collect it for you — free of charge."

"*The Council!*" Rose stared and put down her cup with trembling fingers. "You mean they'll just dispose of it like — *rubbish?*"

The girls exchanged a glance, the kind of glance Rose understood so well. A glance which said quite unmistakably, "Poor Mum. She's so completely out of touch."

"I'm afraid it's the only way," Eileen said gently. "There's not much demand for pianos these days, unless it's fairly new — or old enough to be a real antique."

Aware of an awkward pause, she quickly changed the subject. "Mum, you'll love the flat once you've got used to it. Just think — there'll be no more fires for you to light! You'll find it such a boon, the central heating . . ."

"And think of the time you'll save," Frances added. "No stairs to clean, none of those awkward, dust-collecting corners — and such a pleasant view, just opposite the park . . "

Rose made no answer. She didn't want to think about the future.

She felt her own safe, familiar world slipping away. Soon there'd be nothing left of it, she thought. The ache in her heart was almost physical. To lose the piano would be bad enough . . . but to lose it in such a way!

The girls were still talking brightly, persuasively, about the flat. Rose scarcely heard a word. Couldn't they *see*, she thought. A piano was more than just a clumsy piece of furniture which had outlived its use . . .

And this was her *own* piano, bought with so many hopes and so much pride, soon to be lifted up with careless hands, trundled away unceremoniously and thrown on a pile of scrap.

But all the same, that evening she phoned the local council.

A girl's voice answered. "Name and address, please? Yes, Mrs Prescott, we can pick it up for you. Our men will be collecting in your district between nine and ten tomorrow morning."

Soon it would all be over, Rose thought. An empty space just opposite the window, a strange, light oblong patch where the old fading wallpaper had been protected . . .

THE van was at the gate soon after breakfast, its dark bulk filling up the front room window.

Two men got out. One was young and long haired, dressed in shabby jeans, and he whistled nonchalantly as he loped towards the door. The other was red faced, middle aged and muscular.

Rose opened the door for them in silence. She couldn't even bring herself to say "good morning."

She pointed to the front room door. "Through there . . ." she told them briefly.

She left them then and crept into the kitchen. At least she could spare herself the sight of her piano being prepared for its last humiliating journey.

She waited and listened, but she couldn't hear any sound at all. Why couldn't they take it and be done with it, she wondered. This waiting was almost more than she could bear . . .

"Oh, Mrs Prescott, could you spare a moment?"

She opened the kitchen door. One of the men, the red-faced one, was standing in the hall. He

Continued overleaf

NEW POUNDS FOR OLD

A few months ago, my wife went on a diet and was thrilled to lose quite a lot of weight.

My only complaint?

I've gained all the extra weight that she lost!

She kept forgetting to cook less "starchy" foods. And all the chips, cakes and puddings which she avoided ended up on my plate!

[Bet she wouldn't agree to swap back.]

147

smiled at her and she saw for the first time how kind his eyes were.

"This piano of yours — you've kept it beautiful. It seems a shame that it should go for scrap . . .

"Now Mandy, our youngest girl, she takes these music lessons. Only she has to practise at her gran's, the wife and me not having a piano, see? So I was wondering . . ."

"If you could take it for her? Oh, I do wish you would!"

Rose felt as if a burden had been lifted, a burden much heavier than the old piano. She smiled at him, a smile of pure relief.

"With most of the youngsters nowadays," he added, "it's nothing but compact discs and lasers. But Mandy — well now, she's different, you know."

Rose smiled again — a smile of understanding. "Wait — I've got something else for you," she told him. "It's upstairs in my room. I won't be long."

She plodded up the stairs, panting a little, wishing that she could climb them twice as fast. She found what she wanted in her wardrobe drawer, the drawer where she'd always kept her special treasures, and carried it down with eager, trembling fingers.

The red-faced man was fumbling in his pockets. "I'd like to pay you for the piano," he murmured awkwardly. "Seeing as it's going to be of use, like."

"No, no . . . I mean, I don't want money for it. It's just that I want to feel it's *owned* by someone. Someone who'll use it and take care of it — give it a home. I dare say that sounds foolish . . .

"And I'd like you to have this, too. For your little girl."

He took what she offered him and read aloud, "Six Simple Pieces for the Pianoforte."

His face lit up. "Well, thank you." He beamed. "I'm very much obliged. That'll just suit our Mandy!"

R OSE sat alone that evening in the firelight. She was tired — it had been a long, eventful day. But somehow she felt a strange contentment.

She would be happy in the flat, she thought, once she had settled down. The stairs had been far too much for her these last few months. It wasn't just the cleaning of them either . . .

And, of course, with more time to spare she wouldn't get so tired. She'd go more often to the Women's Institute; perhaps she might even join a pottery class!

And she need never be afraid of loneliness, with the girls and their families popping in so often . . .

She smiled at the empty space against the wall. The piano, too, had found a brand-new home . . .

And one day soon the rooms of a little unknown house in town would ring with the music of "A Dream In Springtime . . ."

———————— * **THE END** * ————————

MY SISTER KATY...

She'd already given up a secure job and drawn her life savings. Now there was some talk of living in a bird cage . . .

MY sister Katy is peculiar. And it's not just me who thinks so. I heard Mum and Dad discussing her over their coffee in the sitting-room only the other day. Due to late-night hunger pangs, I'd been investigating the refrigerator and I was just creeping upstairs with a glass of milk and a sandwich when I heard Dad.

"I never thought a daughter of mine would do such a thing," he said. "Driving all over the country in a beat-up old van, setting up shops in markets all over the place."

Even Mum sounded a bit ruffled. "Well, I suppose she's just going through a stage, dear," she said. "All girls do."

"*You* didn't," Dad pointed out. And in reply Mum gave a sort of complacent giggle.

Complete Story by ELIZABETH ASHCROFT

"You didn't know me at eighteen, Jim. And when I was eighteen I wanted to go and join a circus. Quite fancied myself as a trapeze artiste . . ."

I halted on the second stair. Mum, with her wide, calm smile, and her tweedy skirts and flat shoes, had wanted to join a circus! I didn't believe it. Dad didn't either.

"Humph!" he said after a long silence. "You didn't, though."

"No, but I would have done if my father hadn't forbidden it. I've always regretted it. At least Katy's getting it out of her system while she's young."

"Maybe." There was a thump and I guessed that he'd just put his mug down heavily as a kind of protest. "But she's only just eighteen and I don't like it. It's *odd*. I wish she'd go back to Jones & Son."

I remembered the row they'd had about that. Katy had come home one Friday night, clutching her pay packet, a bunch of flowers for Mum and a box of cigars for Dad. As soon as she came into the sitting-room I knew something was up. So I ducked down behind my geography book and pretended I wasn't there.

"Well, that's that!" Katy said with a sort of brightness that should have warned them. It was summer and she was wearing her working skirt and blouse. In 10 minutes, if she went true to form, she'd be upstairs changing into a beaded kaftan or a maxi with a slit up the side. That was another thing — she dressed odd, my sister, not at all like other boys' sisters I knew.

Mum took the flowers with a pleased smile and Dad took the cigars gingerly, as though he expected them to blow up any minute.

"What do you mean, *that's that?*" he asked, and Katy plumped herself down on the sofa next to Mum and beamed at him.

B UT from behind my book I saw that her eyes were a little wary, and that she was hugging her knees tight, to stop her hands from shaking the way they always did when she was nervous.

"I've handed in my notice," she said firmly. "One more week in the slave galley and then I'm off."

She stopped to take a breath and Dad put down the cigars on the arm of the chair.

"What are you going to do, then? You have to do something. I can't keep you." He was getting angry now and I flinched a little. "You can't just leave your job like that, without even telling us!"

"I have." Katy stood up and stared fixedly at the painting over the fireplace. "I've gone into partnership with Moira. We're starting up a business together."

"Business! Partnership!" Dad was spluttering now. "How can you go into business? You've got no money!"

"I've saved some. I've taken it out of the bank and we've bought a van between us and stocked it up."

"Stocked it up! What with?" Dad was looking anxious now.

"Clothes. We're going to be a travelling boutique. We're going to go to all the local markets and set up a stall. We're going to call ourselves the Wandering Boutique.

That was the start of the row. It went on for all the following week. In the end Katy threatened to leave home, and Mum talked Dad into letting her try it. Finally, he washed his hands of the whole business.

THEN, on the Saturday, Moira brought the van into our drive and they began painting it. Dad was in the greenhouse and wouldn't even come and see it. But I had no such reservations and stopped repairing my broken-down old bike and went to investigate.

Moira and Katy were standing in the drive, hands on hips, admiring it.

"It's beautiful!" Katy said enthusiastically. "Now, where's the paint?"

A WASHOUT!

A few weeks ago I used a special rinse on my hair. Once it was dry, I waited eagerly for my husband to notice the "glowing highlights."

At last he looked up. "Have you washed your hair?"

"Yes," I answered, waiting for some flattering comment.

"Thought so," he grumbled. "Every blooming towel is soaking wet!"

She scurried off into the garage and staggered out with two large cans of paint and assorted brushes. That was when she saw me and started shaking her head firmly.

"Oh, no, Robbie. You're not helping, thank you."

Considering I hadn't even offered, I thought her refusal was a little premature. But I supposed she was thinking about the last time I helped her paint her bedroom. I don't really like thinking about it, but ever since then she's had a purple carpet striped with pink.

"It's outside, Katy," I protested. "So even if I did spill anything it wouldn't matter! Oh, go on, Katy! Please."

I really was longing to have a go. The van wasn't really beautiful, in fact it was a bit fallen-apart looking. There was a streak of rust along the wings, but I was sure I could camouflage that for her.

Moira — who always wore large, round, horn-rimmed glasses and looked a bit owlish, but wasn't — interrupted.

"Katy, we've got three days to get it finished before the first market. If we miss it, we don't make any money, remember?"

Katy looked at her then looked at me and shrugged resignedly.

"OK, then. Grab a paint brush, Robbie. You do the wings — and be careful."

Half an hour later, the van looked completely different. I'd sloshed bright yellow paint all over the wings, which had been a dirty green, and the girls had painted the body bright orange. Then Tim-next-door leaned over the hedge and shouted:

"Hey! What's *that?*"

Katy looked haughty. "It's our van. Remember, I told you about it," she added crossly and he grinned across the hedge.

"*That's* the answer to Mary Quant?"

Katy didn't answer but began slapping on paint angrily. She and Tim were always having arguments and making it up only to fall out again. Everyone expected them to get married one day — except me. And I knew because I'd heard her talking to Moira about him last summer.

"He's more like a brother than anything," she'd been saying, lying under the apple tree. "I mean I've known him ever since I can remember and there isn't any sort of romance or excitement about it."

Moira had pushed her glasses further up her nose and nodded understandingly. They'd been sitting gossiping the way girls do.

I COULDN'T understand girls. I like Tim. He played rugby for the town and was the strongest man I knew. And every so often he'd slip me a fifty-pence piece when he needed help to make it up with Katy.

But now, he was putting his foot right in it. "Like me to drive you down to the market next week? Just to make sure you get there all in one piece?" he asked.

"No thank you!" Katy exploded. "And it's not just Saturdays, Tim. We're driving all over the country. It's a business, a proper business, so stop laughing at it!"

His face fell. "Oh, sorry . . . Well, I just wanted to know if you'd come to a party tonight."

She glowered at him over the paint brush. "Can't, I'm too busy for that kind of thing."

That was it.

Tim took someone else to the party and a few weeks later Moira told Katy that he was serious about the other girl. Katy, who'd said she didn't care what he did, went all pale and dark eyed after that. Even when she was driving round the country with the van full of odd-looking clothes, she looked a little lost, like she'd just left something behind her. Still, they seemed to be doing all right with the business, though.

They'd decided not to call it the Wandering Boutique, after what Dad had said. Instead, they'd called it The Birdcage and Katy had painted a huge pink and orange and yellow bird, like a parrot, on the side.

Inside, they'd got lots of shelves and clothes hanging on rails. There was also a long mirror and a partitioned-off one end with

ZSA ZSA GABOR

★★★★★★★★★★★★★★★

'One young woman asked Zsa Zsa Gabor for help: "I want to break off my engagement to a very wealthy man who has already given me a sable coat, diamonds, a stove and a Rolls-Royce. What should I do?"

Without hesitation Zsa Zsa replied, "Give back the stove."

When asked about her ideal husband, she said, "I want a man who's kind and understanding. Is that too much to ask of a millionaire?"'

★★★★★★★★★★★★★★★★★★★★★

bright yellow curtains so that people could try on clothes. And lots of people did try on clothes. In fact they were so busy they began talking about getting someone else to help.

"But that means splitting the profits!" Moira said crossly. They'd parked the van in our drive and were putting in new stock. I was at a loose end and was hanging around them just waiting for something to crop up. Now something had and I pounced at it eagerly.

"I'm on holiday, Katy! Couldn't I help?"

There was a dead silence, which meant more than a mountain of objections. But I rushed on before they could say anything. "You said it was getting the stall ready you wanted help with. I could do that. I wouldn't want any of the profits . . . Well, just a bit every week."

She grinned suddenly, and when Katy grinned it was difficult not to grin back.

"I thought so! Knew you wouldn't do it for love, anyway!" She turned to Moira. "What do you think? Shall we give him a try?"

THE following Monday I was up early and half an hour later we were bouncing along the main road towards the market. Tim passed us with his girlfriend on his scooter and hooted noisily. Katy ignored him, though she went bright pink.

"She's pretty," I ventured, and she glowered sideways at me.

"Who's pretty?"

"Tim's new girl. I saw him with her yesterday. She's blonde."

"I know," she gritted. "Out of a bottle."

I recognised the danger signs, shut up, and concentrated on looking out the window.

It was super being out so early, there was hardly any traffic on the road. We picked up Moira at her gate, and the sun was out and there

Continued on page 156

THE family that eats together, meets together, and so can discuss the day's events and share in each other's lives. Those families become a closer unit.

On the other hand, families that shop together, flop together, because they wreck the budget, destroy the nervous system and kill the diet.

Those families become poor, irritable and fat.

For that reason shopping is a job that must be done alone, by the most hard-hearted member of the family — the mother. But even though I know what I should do, I cannot always do it.

In spite of my best intentions, there are times when I find myself in the same supermarket with my husband or my children.

You see, because of my various commitments during the week, I'm very often forced to do the bulk of my shopping on Saturday morning, when my husband is home from work, so I do get caught.

I try not to let him know too far in advance that I'm planning to go to the supermarket. For instance, as I walk out the door I call out, "See you later! I'm going shopping."

And before he knows what's happening, I'm gone.

Sometimes, though, my husband beats me to it. "Dear," he announces when looking for a snack, "we don't seem to have any pickled onions. Shouldn't we go shopping some time soon?"

And so, because of circumstances beyond my control, my husband and I start out on our trip to the supermarket together. Once we get inside the store, I have to keep my wits about me.

I not only have to see to it that I get all the items on my list, check-

Buy, Buy

I know there are women who can calmly undertake a visit to the supermarket, shop sensibly and buy just what they need. But then, says Roni Borden, these lucky ladies don't have a family like mine . . .

ing comparative prices while I do it, but I have to discuss the value of all the television-advertised foods with my husband, and, at the same time, give him some idea of our budget limitations.

OUR tour of the supermarket usually starts at my husband's favourite place — the meat counter.

"We haven't had a steak in long time," he says, a pathetically hopeful note in his voice.

"That's because everyone seems to want a meal every night in the week," I answer firmly. "As soon as you're ready to fast for an evening or two, I'd be happy to get us a steak."

My husband's next favourite aisle is the cake and pie section. At this point I try to get him past with some stimulating conversation.

"Did you hear the latest gossip about Nancy and Ralph?"

"Gossip? You know I don't like gossip. What is it, anyway?"

"Well, when Ralph goes off to work in the morning . . ."

With any luck, by the time I've relayed the gossip, we've passed all the cakes and pies and are turning into the next aisle.

Blues !

"Doesn't that apricot nectar look interesting?" he will say.

"You mean the one we couldn't even get the dog to finish last year?" I respond, like lightning.

In spite of all my fancy side-stepping, though, I still have to inspect everything that goes from the trolley on to the check-out counter.

You see, although my husband has a way of appearing to agree with me or to be sidetracked by me, he still sneaks extra little goodies into the trolley as soon as my back is turned.

BUT if shopping with my husband is a battle of wits, shopping with my children is a battle of nerves.

But there are days when I have to take my children shopping with me to help carry the stuff. To begin with, they're not very keen.

"You need a new pair of shoes," I announce to my son.

"Great!" he says. "I'm finally going to get those terrific trainers."

Then he'll decide that trainers aren't worth a trip to the supermarket.

However, once I get my children inside the supermarket, they do manage to make the best of things. They get their own trolley and start off by going over to the confectionery aisle for a good look.

Having made their selection from the sweets, their next stop is the potato crisps and peanuts aisle, where they pick up one box of each size and brand.

Next they pick up a few containers of whipped cream, several litres of ice-cream and some tubs of frozen dessert.

Having done that, the kids are finished their shopping and are ready to leave. *Continued overleaf*

155

Continued from previous page

I 'VE found the only way to get the kids to stop nagging me for permission to go to the check-out at this point, with only the foods in their trolley, is to stand in the middle of the vegetable aisle.

My children treat the vegetable aisle as though it were ringed with smallpox.

And, of course, there is my son's favourite section, the one that displays all the junk toys and oddments.

"You can look at them," I state very clearly and emphatically, "but I do not intend to buy you anything from that rack."

"I know you don't," he says in a rather adult manner. "I'm just looking."

An hour later, I drag him out of the supermarket, yelling.

"But my friend Jeff has a toy diver and I need one to put in my bath."

Following him are my daughters, who whisper at the tops of their lungs, "It's such a shame that our mother is too mean to buy proper food for us."

I keep my head down as I race for the car, missing half the items I planned to buy, but happy to be out of the store.

Although I shall probably continue to suffer the difficulties of shopping, I do have the perfect solution to the entire problem.

I could eliminate my shopping headaches and cut down on the children's between-meal snacks at the same time.

I haven't yet convinced my husband of the worth of my plan — but what's wrong with eating every meal in a restaurant . . . ■

Continued from page 153
was a sort of fresh warm hay smell in the air. I didn't remember ever being up and out so early.

"It's fabulous!" I shouted in glee, but just then Katy shot round a large lorry and screeched in front of it.

As we'd flashed past I'd seen that the lorry was filled with old tatty furniture, bits of beds, and there was a big sofa with stuffing curling out of it.

The driver honked furiously at us and Katy honked back.

Moira peered back at the lorrry. "Bet that's going to the market," she said. Sure enough, it was — right next to our pitch.

The market was filled with rushing, shouting people, all putting up stalls, with bright red and blue and yellow canopies, and piling up boxes of goods and fruit and just plain junk. I felt a pang of pride when I saw what Katy and Moira were doing. They were actually making a sort of birdcage round their stall with bits of bamboo . . .

Katy saw me just standing gaping and grabbed me.

"Come on, Robbie. Just tack these bits of bamboo on to the canopy and then Moira will give you the parrots and swings and you can put them up."

Moira was delving into the large box she'd held on her knee all the way. She brought out three large brightly-coloured parrots with large curved yellow beaks and long feathery tails, sitting on little swings.

"I made them," she said briefly, seeing my awed expression. "Here you are, Robbie. Hang them over the counter, then it'll really look like a birdcage."

In half an hour we were all ready. The stall was a blaze of sparkly blouses and shirts and pants and long swishy skirts, and the van doors were open and things were hanging on the rails inside.

Katy disappeared into the van and came out dressed differently. I gasped when I saw what she had on. She was wearing a long patchwork skirt which I recognised as a quilt my grandma had made and which used to be on Katy's bed. It was a family heirloom, sort of, and I bet Mum didn't know where it had finished up.

A lacy shawl was draped around her shoulders and she'd let her hair down from its sort of bun so that it hung all loose on her shoulders.

She looked as though she was going to a party. Moira was all dressed up, too, in a smock affair with flowers all over it.

"OK," Katy said briskly. "We're off . . . Can I help you?" she said, turning to a tall fair-haired young man who was peering at her through the bars of the birdcage.

"Yes, you can!" he began angrily. "You ought to be had up for dangerous driving. You nearly had me in the ditch just now!"

I saw he was very tall and dressed in old jeans and a pinky-purply shirt. His hands weren't very clean, and when he rubbed his forehead in a bewildered way he left some dust on it.

"You nearly ran me off the road an hour ago with your van. Or, should I say, this apology of a van! You nearly had me *and* all my furniture in the ditch!"

"Oh, so that was you, was it?" Katy's face cleared. "Well, you *didn't* go into the ditch, so everything's all right, then, isn't it? Now, if you'll excuse me, I have a customer."

And she left him, still muttering away under his breath.

THAT was the first time I met Sam Brent. After that, every time we went to a market and set up our stall, he seemed to be next to us. Katy ignored him, and Moira, who'd just found a new boyfriend, wasn't interested in him. But I liked him.

Sometimes when we weren't busy I'd look at his stall, which had lots of little tables and chairs and sometimes sofas, with buttons falling off the back.

"Junk!" Katy said scornfully, when I mentioned how good it all looked.

"High-class furniture, it says," I said, staring at the lettering on the van.

"Junk," she said again, and turned away. Then I bumped into Sam as he was taking coffee and buns back to his pitch.

"Look out!" he yelped, and coffee cascaded down his jeans. Then he saw it was me and grinned. "Hi! You're the boy from the parrot cage, aren't you?"

I grinned back. "Sorry," I said.

Ten minutes later I was sitting behind his stall on a rickety old chair eating a sugary doughnut. His stuff was more interesting to me than the girls' clothes, and I picked up a chipped china dragon and looked at it curiously.

"Like it?" he asked proudly, and I nodded wistfully.

The summer seemed to be settling into a routine now, and I was getting a little bored. Tim's engagement had been announced and ever since then, Katy had been a bit pale and wan looking. I saw Sam watching her.

"Shouldn't have thought your sister would like this sort of life," he observed.

He was watching Sally again. "Robbie, look after the shop for a minute, will you? If anyone asks, everything's been priced."

I watched him go with my mouth open and he disappeared round the side of the Jellied Eels and the Sweet Stall. Five minutes later he returned carrying two steaming mugs of coffee and some buns. Both of which he plonked down in front of Katy.

"Compliments of the next-door management," he said, and stood beaming down at her.

Katy looked up from a dress she was folding, her eyes squinting into the sunlight. Even then she couldn't have seen proprly because the hand she raised to protect her from the sun caught one of the mugs and sent it flying — all over a pile of sweaters.

"Oh, no!" she moaned. "Now look what you've done! You — you idiot!"

Sam, standing under a swinging parrot, looked upset. "Oh, I'm sorry. I'd no idea — I mean, well, you knocked it over yourself!" he began.

But Katy was in no mood for apologies. She picked up the sticky buns and pushed them towards him.

"I don't *want* your old iced buns or your coffee!" she spluttered. "Take them away! You've ruined half the stock! And send Robbie back at once. He's supposed to be helping me, not you!"

He came back slowly, a rueful expression on his face. "Well, that little peace offering didn't work, did it?"

"Never mind," I said and pushed 75 pence into his hand. "I sold your old dragon for you. I'd better go — she's a bit cross."

SO reluctantly I went back to Katy, who was piling up the sweaters and grumbling loudly.

"We'll have to have a sale," she was muttering. "Or mark them down as seconds, or something . . . why doesn't he find a pitch somewhere else! I'm tired of having his old junk next to us. It spoils the tone of The Birdcage!"

I told that to Sam later but he just laughed.

"Old junk!" he echoed. "They're antiques, some of them. This mug is a hundred years old! Your sister has no idea what junk is!"

That was when Katy, running from the back of the van round to serve someone, tripped over an old warming pan Sam had put on the ground. She landed with a dull clang on top of it, knocking over a large painted china jug which shattered loudly against a chair.

Sam and I found her sitting on the ground, her face all red with what I imagined to be a mixture of anger and embarrassment.

She was mad — *really* mad.

"Why can't you put your things where people can't fall over them?" she stormed. "I've torn my skirt on your rotten old frying-pan!"

"Frying-pan! *Frying-pan!* That's a bed warmer, you nincompoop."

Sam was furious. "You've also broken a valuable jug, Katy Birdcage!"

THEY didn't speak to each other for ages after that. Sam set up his stuff in an injured silence and ignored me, too, which hurt. And Katy and Moira ostentatiously hung signs over the pile of sweaters which had been cleaned. *Shop Soiled, Half Price,* they said. They were hung in such a way that Katy made sure Sam could see it from his pitch.

Then Moira got engaged.

All of a sudden she was getting married . . . and wanting to take out her money in The Birdcage and stop being Katy's partner.

"Oh, but you can't!" Katy protested when we'd just finished clearing up for the day. It was September now and getting chilly.

WATER-BED!

When I owned a house not far from the beach, I used to spread seaweed as fertiliser among my vegetables and flowers.

The time came to sell the house, and I just couldn't understand why none of the interested viewers made an offer.

I eventually discovered the reason, however, when one couple asked anxiously, "How often does the tide come up as far as your garden?"

There were even a few stalls selling Christmas presents and cards. And I was now only helping on Saturday because of school.

I'd been sitting on the counter under the flapping red canopy reading a comic, and when I heard Katy's voice, I looked up and listened silently.

"Katy, I'm sorry," Moira said again. "But John — well, he says it's a — a funny sort of thing for a girl to do, anyway. And I need the money, for things for the flat. I'm sorry, Katy, but you'll find someone else, I'm sure."

"How?" Katy asked gloomily. "Advertise? Who would be daft enough?" she added. Her tone made me wonder if she wasn't enjoying The Birdcage so much now it was nearly autumn.

"It's a good business," Moira said stoutly. "I've loved doing it, you

Continued on page 162

SQUEAK

When we found him he was starving. But it wasn't long before we were eating out of *his* hand!

SQUEAK was born about May 24, 1960, and then abandoned on the bank of a loch in Scotland.

Our youngest son, Mervyn, then fourteen years old, had spent the day fishing at the loch and arrived home in the evening, soaked to the skin.

From his pocket, he produced a tiny little animal like a mouse, equally soaked, and nearly dead.

Luckily, I had a nice cosy fire burning, and while the little animal dried out, I got some warm milk with two drops of brandy in it. We had to force its little mouth open and get it to swallow some of the warm mixture.

After a while, the little creature began to show signs of life. However, we knew we couldn't leave it, so we all took turn about of feeding it and keeping it warm through the night.

By morning, we were all so happy that he was still alive. We examined him closely and came to the conclusion he must be a baby otter.

We continued feeding him warm milk and brandy and as he grew steadily stronger, he was promoted to switched egg and milk, then cod liver oil, then bread, milk and raw fish.

By June 12, his eyes were open and he knew us all and would squeak with excitement when we spoke to him. We decided to call him Squeak!

We kept him in a big box in the kitchen, one part filled with fresh hay, and an old woolly jersey for him to sleep on, the other to play in, and a

ramp, to run out and in as he liked. He was very clean, and had no smell.

By this time, he was one of the family, and knew all my movements. It was a great thrill the first time he popped out of his box in the morning, and followed me around the house, chittering and chattering, just as though he had missed me, and was pleased to see me again.

AT that time, we lived in an upstairs flat, with an inside staircase to ourselves. One day, I had some washing to hang out, and hurried along the lobby, and was down two steps when I heard a squeak behind me.

There was Squeak, doing his best to come down the steps.

But he couldn't quite make it, and was so annoyed and frustrated, I picked him up and took him down to the back garden with me.

About a week later, he managed to go downstairs by himself, he was proud of his achievement. The excitement and chattering was terrific!

The only time I was allowed out of his sight was when he grew sleepy. Then he would disappear quietly into his box and sleep for an hour or two, like a kitten, or a pup, then out he would pop, ready for more mischief.

If I sat in a chair, he would climb up on to my knee, then up to my shoulder and run round my neck, nibbling at each ear, then he would

Mink In A Million

give me a kiss and run down again. I never thought it possible for anyone to get such a lot of love and affection from a wild animal.

BY this time he was four months old and still growing. We still thought he was an otter, and wondered what we should do with him in a council house, if he grew to be two to three feet long. It wasn't till later that we discovered our "otter" was a mink.

Meanwhile, we had many visitors. Parents would bring their children and, though many weren't sure of Squeak at first, they soon got over their misgivings when they saw how friendly and soft he was.

Eventually, we enquired about getting him admitted to Edinburgh Zoo. He had given us so much happiness and fun, it was heartbreaking to part with him, but we wanted him to be safe, somewhere where he would be properly fed and looked after.

His new master had a big box ready for him on the porch. We put Squeak in there with his jersey and his own toys. He soon settled down and went to sleep, and we were able to leave.

NEXT time I saw Squeak, he heard me walking up the drive towards his enclosure, and went mad with excitement when I called to him. He clung to the netting of his enclosure and chattered away. He had grown to the size of a cat.

I went inside to be with him, and he gave me such a welcome. He ran up his sloping ramp and jumped on to my shoulder and nibbled at my ears, giving me a kiss like he used to do. I hadn't seen him for six months, but he remembered me.

That was the last time I saw Squeak. Soon after, he escaped.

We have one consolation. Squeak was happy while he lived. He gave lots of people a lot of pleasure, and I'm sure there will never be another pet like him. We'll never forget him. ■

L

Continued from page 159
know I have. It's just — well — I'll have a husband to look after soon."

Sam went by, half-hidden under a wooden chair with a cane seat. The cane was unravelling and trailing behind him. I got down and picked it up and helped him with the chair.

"Thanks." He turned to me, grinning, puffing a bit. "What's the argument?"

"Moira's getting married," I told him. "She wants her bit of the partnership back."

"Oh. That means trouble," he said. And when he turned to pick up a large oil lamp he'd dropped he walked straight into Katy, who was coming round the other side of the van.

"Ouch!" She almost dropped a pile of dresses, and he straightened and stood staring down at her.

There was a funny sort of silence. Then I saw with horror that she had tears in her eyes. Katy never, ever cried.

"Oh, you again!" she blurted out. "Why can't you leave me alone?" And in a flurry of skirts she disappeared into the van and slammed the door.

I picked up the pile of clothes and gave them to Moira.

"She's — a bit upset," Moira said to Sam apologetically.

Sam got into his lorry and sat for a moment before driving off.

Katy drove home in silence. We overtook Sam's lorry on a bend and she hooted noisily at him. I saw Sam staring angrily down at us, then there was a funny clattering sort of noise and he swerved and the last thing I saw he was standing looking angrily down at a tyre and kicking it.

"He could have had us over," Moira cried and Katy didn't say anything and I wondered what she was going to do.

WE soon found out. The next Saturday she banged on my bedroom door earlier than usual.

"Come on, Robbie! I'm going early today!"

I stumbled out half-asleep. It was bitterly cold and for once I didn't want to go. Then she drove straight past Moira's gate.

"What about Moira?" I asked blankly, and she turned a set face to me.

"She's left," she said. "I'm on my own now."

When we got to the market it was so cold I couldn't stop shivering. I got the stall ready and then went to get some coffee. Suddenly I wished I were home in bed and Katy was back at Jones & Son.

Then about twelve o'clock it started — the biggest, worst rainstorm I'd ever seen.

Suddenly, the market was deserted except for scurrying, grumbling stall-holders, rushing with their merchandise to their vans and cars and pushing things to shelter. The puddles grew bigger and bigger every minute.

Katy was running backwards and forwards, arms full of clothes, and I was struggling with the parrots on their swings, when I was suddenly aware that Katy was crying. Her face was covered in tears and rain, her lovely quilted skirt dragging in the mud, and her hair in wet straggly wisps round her face.

"Oh, it's awful, awful!" she moaned. "I wish I hadn't started. If only Moira hadn't left!"

Sam, next door, had loaded up his lorry and was just going to swing into the driving seat when there was a terrible roaring sound, and our stall just collapsed. On top of Katy.

"Katy!" Sam was there in seconds, and we were scrabbling in the rain and under the billowing canopy and bamboo canes for her.

"Katy!" Sam kept bellowing, heaving planks of wood out of the way as if they were matches.

THEN we saw her, all crumpled up, with a pile of skirts in her arms. There were tears streaking her cheeks, and her eyes were huge and blue and wet.

Sam scooped her up and stood, a sequinned blouse dangling from his shoulders, and just looked down at her in the rain.

"Are you all right?"

"I — I think so." She didn't sound like Katy at all. Just very shaken and lost. "I — bumped my head."

"It's only a scratch," he said, stroking it.

The wind had died down a little, but her skirt was billowing round them and I felt sort of in the way somehow. We were just standing there, silent, in the middle of the empty market square, with the rain pouring down all around us.

"You nearly killed me last week," he said suddenly. I got worried then in case he was going to get mad with her and drop her, but then I saw Katy's eyes were on his, and a little smile dimpling her cheeks.

"You made me angry," she said. Then suddenly her arms were round his neck. "But I wouldn't have hurt you for anything. You know that."

I don't know how he knew, but he was nodding away. Suddenly, they were both beaming widely at each other.

I just stood with the rain streaming down my face, thinking they'd both gone mad. Then, to my utter astonishment, Sam was kissing her.

Blushing furiously, I shot into the van. I didn't understand it, any of it. I thought they hated each other.

Katy's given up The Birdcage now. She's working with Sam, in his antique shop. Some Saturdays she goes along with him to his stall in the market, where he sells off the old stuff he can't get rid of in the shop.

I go along and help sometimes. Mum and Dad still think she's peculiar, but I don't.

Sam makes a smashing brother-in-law . . .

——————— * **THE END** * ———————

THROUGH THE

The first time he met her he'd known this was the girl for him. The hard part was convincing her that he was right . . .

Complete Story By
EILEEN ELIAS

IT was pouring rain as Fergus Grant reached the City Art School. Running the last hundred yards, he dashed for cover.

Safely inside out of the wet, he shook his dripping umbrella and discarded his raincoat. Then he rushed up the stairs to the first-floor studio — the one where the night-school class was held.

It wasn't exactly easy — not with a portfolio under one arm and his painting gear under the other. But if he didn't hurry, somebody else from Mr Bennett's Recreational Painting Class might beat him to the place he wanted — the easel next to Sally Marshall.

Fergus plunged through the swing doors, and immediately most of his painting gear crashed

EYES OF LOVE

the floor, brushes and tubes of paint rolling everywhere. Miss Marshall, already calmly seated t her easel, looked up with faint ritation.

"Sorry!" Fergus apologised, crabbling furiously under a able. He retrieved a handful of rushes, and, straightening himelf, looked at Miss Marshall ith a rueful smile.

"It's that stupid swing door," he explained. "Nobody can ever get through it without dropping all their stuff."

"I can," said Miss Marshall primly, and went on squeezing tubes of paint on to her palette.

Snubbed, Fergus set up his canvas on the easel next to hers. He was always being snubbed by Sally Marshall.

Out of the corner of his eye he studied her. Pale gold hair, pulled back with a rubber band so that it wouldn't interfere with her work. It would look lovely, Fergus thought, if only she'd let it spread out over her shoulders. Blue-grey eyes, a serious little profile, and, he was sure, the slimmest of slim figures hidden beneath that appalling old blue smock of hers.

The trouble was, she'd never given him a chance to see her in anything else but that shapeless overall.

He tried again. "Filthy night outside," he said. "Raining cats and dogs."

"I wouldn't know," said Miss Marshall calmly. "It wasn't raining when I left home. But of course I was early."

Snubbed again, thought Fergus. Sally Marshall was *always* early. Indeed he had sometimes wondered if she ever went home at all from Friday night to Friday night. First to arrive, she was always last to go, too.

FERGUS had hung about every Friday for nearly a term, hoping to walk her home, but Miss Marshall always made some excuse.

She'd stay deep in conversation with old Mr Bennett, the tutor, or chat to the two Miss Simmonds.

Indeed, if it hadn't been for the two Miss Simmonds, Fergus told himself, he wouldn't even have known Miss Marshall's christian name. It had been on the second Friday of term that Fergus, finding himself sharing a canteen table in the coffee break with them, had introduced the subject of the absent Miss Marshall.

"That young lady next to me upstairs," he'd said, toying with his spoon. "Doesn't she ever have a break for coffee?"

The two Miss Simmonds had given each other meaningful looks.

"She did all last year," volunteered Miss Gladys.

"But not this year," added Miss Sybil.

"Well, what's different about this year?" persisted Fergus.

"Last year," Miss Sybil said in a low voice, "we had young Mr Reilly here."

"Who's Mr Reilly?" Fergus asked impatiently.

Miss Sybil had leaned forward. "Mr Reilly was our tutor last year. He and Miss Marshall used to get on very well together. In fact, at one time," she looked at Miss Gladys, "we thought that there might be a little romance in our art class. Then at the end of the summer Mr Reilly left to take up a teaching job up north somewhere. Since then Sarah's not been the same."

Sarah, Fergus had thought. So that was her name. He didn't think it suited her. He'd decided to call her Sally instead.

"It was such a pity," Miss Sybil had said. "And this year — well, she won't join in like she used to do. Simply lives for her painting. I had a word with her only last week. From now on, she says, she's going to be wedded to her art."

"Wedded to her aunt?" Fergus's eyebrows had shot up.

" 'Art,' I said," Miss Sybil explained patiently. "Just a phrase. But it's quite obvious — at least to us — that Sarah is a changed person. That's why she doesn't come down for coffee with us, I suppose."

Fergus had finished his coffee and joined the others as they climbed the stairs to the first-floor studio. Wedded to her art indeed. He'd see about that.

Though usually Fergus was very good at seeing about things, he hadn't been able, so far, to see about Sally.

A whole term had gone by and still they weren't even using christian names. Which was why tonight, waiting for old Mr Bennett to come and begin the last class of term, Fergus had his mouth set in a determined line. If Miss Marshall was ever to become Sarah — let alone Sally — tonight was the night.

THE class was assembled now, easels in place, painting gear set up, and all eyes focused on Mr Bennett.

While the rain battered at the studio windows outside, Fergus wondered briefly what young Mr Reilly had been like. Certainly not in the least like old Bennett there, already polishing his spectacles and beaming genially round the room.

Mr Bennett confronted his class. "Well," he was saying, "I'm pleased to see a turn-out like this on such a nasty night. Most gratifying. I'm glad, too, because this is the last class of term, and I've got a little surprise for you all."

A small stir ran round the class. "This term," Mr Bennett continued, "we've covered a little landscape painting, some still life, one or two life studies and we've tried our hand at portrait painting. Some of you seem quite promising there.

"Now tonight I thought we'd have a little competition in portrait painting." He looked round the room with a smile. "And, as this is
Continued overleaf

☆ ☆

NOEL COWARD

★ ★ ★ ★ ★ ★ ★ ★ ★ ★ ★ ★   ★

‘ Noel Coward was in Hollywood when he heard that a very dim actor, an acquaintance of his, had committed suicide.

"How did he kill himself?" Coward asked.

"Shot his brains out," came the reply.

"He must have been a marvellous shot," was Coward's response. ’

★ ★ ★ ★ ★ ★ ★ ★ ★ ★ ★ ★   ★

Continued from previous page
our last lesson, I will award a small prize to the student whose painting you all consider the best."

Fergus coughed. "Er — whose portrait are we going to paint?" he enquired. "There isn't a model —"

"You're going to paint each other," explained Mr Bennett. "Will you kindly arrange yourselves in pairs and arrange your easels so that you each have some kind of view of your neighbour. Side, front or half-face. Right? You can start whenever you're ready."

Fergus shot a look at his neighbour. Pale gold hair, delicate profile — Sally would make a lovely portrait. What did it matter if he didn't win — it was a chance in a million to keep looking at her!

He shifted his easel so that he had Miss Marshall in good view. He caught her eye and grinned. "Guess that means us," he said.

Miss Marshall, taken by surprise, actually smiled. Just for a second it lit up those serious blue-grey eyes. Fergus grinned triumphantly. It had really happened, the dedicated Miss Marshall had actually smiled!

He hummed cheerfully as he took some paint on his brush and started to rough in her face. Then he stood back and examined, first his sketch and then its subject.

MISS MARSHALL met his glance. Then, wrinkling her nose and holding her brush in mid-air, began to do calculations about the length of Fergus's jawline. Fergus pulled a face at her, but this time there was no answering smile.

"Not bad, Mr Grant," Mr Bennett told him, looking at the nearly-finished portrait just before coffee break. "Not bad at all. If I may say so, you have a definite flair for portrait painting. Keep it up, Mr Grant, keep it up."

Fergus studied his work. To his mind it was just a formal portrait of a formal person. No life in it. It was Sarah, and he wanted Sally.

Mr Bennett passed on, and gazed thoughtfully at Miss Marshall's work. "Mmm," he said, and moved away.

Fergus managed to steal a quick look at Sarah's painting. It was recognisably him, and carefully done, but he had to admit that Sarah Marshall wasn't one of Mr Bennett's star pupils.

"Sorry you've got such an unpromising subject," said Fergus with a lopsided grin. "Afraid I'm no oil painting."

He was hoping for another smile. He was disappointed.

Fergus lifted his aching arms above his head and stretched. Painting was tiring work. "Not joining us for coffee today?" he asked.

Miss Marshall shook her head. "I've a lot to do yet."

"Miss Marshall," Fergus said gravely. "Don't you *ever* feel you'd like a break?"

Sarah returned his gaze. "Not really," she said.

Fergus sighed and followed the others through the swing doors.

Continued on page 170

Santa's S.O.S

by Bruce Andrews

It looked like Christmas would be bleak,
For Rudolph had retired last week.
And Santa couldn't find a way
To hire some help to pull his sleigh.

And then on Christmas Eve he cheered,
Another reindeer had appeared.
"Tell me your name," old Santa cried.
The reindeer shyly stood and sighed.

"It's simply, Simon," Simon said.
"I'm young and strong, but not well read."
But Santa smilingly said, "Stay!
"You don't need brains to pull a sleigh."

He harnessed Simon up, and soon
They sauntered slowly past the moon.
With eyes cast down to pierce the night,
The houses came within their sight.

Then Santa gave the sleigh a smack.
"Oh dear," said he, "we've left the sack."
And Simon's shiny nose turned blue.
He'd no idea what to do.

"It's simple, Simon," Santa said.
"With all these children safe in bed,
"You nip straight back to North Pole State,
"They'll never know that I've been late."

So Simon sped to Santa's scene.
But halfway there he met a dream.
And Ethel Reindeer wasn't slow,
For woman's lib. to strike a blow.

With fluttering eyelids cast his way,
She winked at him without delay.
A promise — generous to a fault.
So Simon slithered to a halt.

It's human nature after all,
To answer quickly love's sweet call.
Well, flying reindeers don't abound.
And lady reindeers can't be found!

So Simon said, "I say, sweet soul,
"Come fly with me up to The Pole.
"We'll quickly pick up Santa's sack.
"No time at all, an' we'll be back."

He sort of nibbled Ethel's ear,
She acquiesced — he gave a cheer.
Though snow, by now, was falling thick,
They did the journey double quick.

Well, Santa sighed with heartfelt joy,
And soon forgave young Simon's ploy.
He sped about with zealous dash,
Dispensing presents in a flash.

He took to Ethel right away,
And told her with them she could stay.
So Santa's family grew — and how!
And Simon's not so simple now . . .

Continued from page 168

"I heard what Mr Bennett was saying to you," chirped Miss Gladys as they sat sipping their coffee. "It's not the first time he's admired your work, Mr Grant."

Miss Sybil nodded. "You've a real flair for portraits, Mr Grant. I shouldn't be surprised if you won the prize."

Fergus felt himself blushing. Hastily he swallowed the rest of his coffee and rushed back up the stairs. Sarah Marshall was still sitting where he'd left her. If she'd looked at his portrait of her, she never gave a sign.

It was nearly a quarter to nine when Mr Bennett announced to the class that time was up. The Miss Simmonds twittered nervously as they made last-minute additions to their work. Fergus, stealing a look at the corner easel, saw Sarah Marshall stand back from her work, and rub a weary hand across her forehead.

Poor girl, he thought, she looks so tired. He glanced again. A streak of Prussian blue was smeared across her forehead.

He studied his portrait again. If only he could catch her just as she looked now — an ordinary girl. She'd turned from Sarah to Sally, tired from an evening's painting. At last, with a streak of Prussian blue on her forehead that she didn't even know was there, she looked human, and approachable.

Fergus took a quick decision. Brush in hand, he reached for his palette and the Prussian blue . . .

"Now, if you please," Mr Bennett was saying, "we've only a few minutes. Will you all bring your portraits forward and prop them against the wall."

ONE by one, canvases were lifted off easels and carried to the front of the studio. Sarah, carefully carrying hers by the edges, set it in the least conspicuous place. Fergus, close behind her, plonked his boldly down next to hers.

She gave a little gasp. "Oh, Mr Grant — do you see what you've done?"

Fergus lifted an eyebrow.

"It was so nice," she went on, "but look, you've smudged it with blue paint."

"What's this?" Mr Bennett was peering over her shoulder. "An accident, Mr Grant? Think nothing of it. It only needs a touch to clean it up."

He picked up a rag and was just about to remove the offending streak when Fegus laid a hand on his arm.

"Excuse me, Mr Bennett. I — meant it to be like that," he said firmly.

Mr Bennett stepped back in surprise. "What's that, Mr Grant? You can't have a fine painting ruined like that. I can get that mark off in a jiffy."

"I don't want it off," Fergus said stubbornly.

"You don't —?" Mr Bennett, nonplussed, took off his spectacles and polished them in irritation. Fergus stood his ground.

"I'm sorry, sir, but that's the way I see my subject. Just as she is now."

Mr Bennett looked from Fergus to Sarah and back again, then shrugged. There was a murmur from the other students. Fergus glanced at Sarah. She had turned slightly pink, he noticed, and her eyes were fixed on him with a bewildered look.

Mr Bennett turned to his class. "In that case, there is nothing further to be said. I'm sorry to see a good piece of work — a very good piece of work — spoiled, by what I can only call an act of — er — wilfulness. But if that is the way Mr Grant wants it," Mr Bennett was polishing his spectacles furiously now, "will you kindly, ladies and gentleman, study the other portraits here and I will abide by your decision."

Fergus did not get the prize. As he joined in the polite applause for the winner he noticed Sarah look at him curiously.

HOLIDAY HITCHES

Whilst travelling on a local bus I overhead a women telling her friend that she had booked her family's summer holiday.

"Although," she added, "I don't really like going on holiday — I never settle in a strange bed. And then Wayne, the youngest, usually gets car-sick. And my oldest boy always comes out in a rash when he goes in the sun. And Father always complains about the cooking!"

"Why do you bother going away then?" her friend asked.

"Well," came the reply, "it makes a change!"

Later, when she and Fergus were washing their brushes side by side at the studio sink, she said, "You know, you should have let Mr Bennett take out that mark. To miss the prize, for a silly little mistake —"

"It wasn't a mistake," Fergus said, scraping off his palette. "That's the way I see you. Or at least, the way I'd like to see you."

She paused, up to her elbows in water, and stared at him. "What do you mean, the way you'd like to see me?"

"I like you best," said Fergus, amazed at his own audacity, "with a bit of Prussian blue. It's still there, some of it, and you've no idea what a difference it makes. It turns you into a real person, not just another art student. It makes you untidy and charming and — well, Sally."

At last he'd said it.

Fergus stopped, half expecting her to look furious, but she didn't. She merely turned a little pinker as she rubbed her handkerchief over her forehead.

Suddenly she smiled. "Oh, Fergus, you're *impossible!*"

Continued on page 174

Cotton on to Crochet

Materials Required. — Of **Patons Cotton Top,** 9 (9, 10, 11, 11) x 50 gram balls; 3.50 mm crochet hook.

For best results it is essential to use the recommended yarn. If you have difficulty in obtaining the yarn, write direct, enclosing a stamped addressed envelope, to the following address for stockists: Customer Liaison Department, Patons & Baldwins, Kilncraigs, Alloa, Clackmannanshire FK10 1EG.

Measurements. — To fit bust — 81 (86, 91, 97, 102) cm, *32 (34, 36, 38, 40) inch;* length from shoulders — 62 (63, 65, 66 67) cm, *24½ (24¾, 25½, 26, 26½) inches;* sleeve seam — 43 cm, *17 inches.*

To team up equally well with trousers or skirt, this sweater, in a pure cotton yarn, uses the simplest of stitches.

Tension. — 17 stitches and 20 rows to 10 cm, *4 inches,* measured over double crochet. 6 treble Vs and 8 rows to 10 cm, *4 inches,* measured over main pattern.

Abbreviations. — Ch. — chain; s.s. — slip stitch; d.c. — double crochet; tr. — treble; st.(s) — stitch(es); V grp.(s) — V group(s) consisting of (1 tr., 1 ch., 1 tr.) all into one st.

N.B. Figures in brackets ( ) refer to the larger sizes; where only one figure is given, this refers to all sizes.

V tr. pattern:

Base row. — 3 ch. (to serve as first tr. and each row started thus), miss next d.c., *1 V grp. in next d.c., miss 2 d.c., repeat from * to last 3 d.c., 1 V grp. in next d.c., miss next d.c., 1 tr. in last d.c.

Pattern row. — 3 ch., *1 V grp. in centre ch. of next V grp., repeat from * to end. 1 tr. in last tr.

This last row forms pattern and is repeated throughout.

Back.

With 3.50 mm crochet hook, make 67 (71, 75, 81, 85) ch.

1st row. — 1 d.c. in 2nd ch. from hook, 1 d.c. in each ch. to end. [66 (70, 74, 80, 84) d.c.]

2nd row. — 1 ch. (as first d.c.), 1 d.c. in each d.c. to end.

Repeat the 2nd row until work measures 7 cm, *2¾ inches.*

Increase row. — 1 ch., 1 d.c. in each of next 0 (4, 1, 9, 11) d.c., *2 d.c. in next d.c., 1 d.c. in each of next 4 (3, 4, 4, 4) d.c., repeat from * 12 (14, 13, 13, 12) times more, 2 d.c. in next d.c., 1 d.c. in each d.c. to end. [80 (86, 89, 95, 98) d.c.]

Repeat 2nd row once more.

Work in V tr. pattern (see abbreviations) throughout, until Back measures 43 cm, *17 inches,* from beginning. Lengthen or shorten here if required.

Mark armholes by marking both ends of last row with a piece of contrast coloured yarn**. Work straight in pattern until work measures 19 (20, 22, 23, 24) cm, *7½ (8, 8¾, 9, 9½) inches,* from markers.

Shape Shoulders.

Next row. — S.s. over first 12 (14, 14, 15, 15) sts., pattern to last 12 (14, 14, 15, 15) sts., turn.

Next row. — S.s. over first 13 (14, 14, 16, 16) sts., pattern to last 13 (14, 14, 16, 16) sts.

Fasten off.

Front.

Work as for Back to **.

Work straight until Front measures 13 (14, 16, 17, 18) cm, *5 (5½, 6¼, 6¾, 7) inches,* from markers.

Shape Neck.

Next row. — Work first 33 (36, 36, 39, 39) sts., turn and work this side first, keeping pattern correct throughout.

Next row. — S.s. over first 3 sts., work to end.

Next row. — Pattern 28 (31, 31, 34, 34) sts., turn.

Decrease 1 st. at neck edge on next 3 rows. [25 (28, 28, 31, 31) sts.]

Work straight until Front measures 19 (20, 22, 23, 24) cm, *7½ (8, 8¾, 9, 9½) inches,* from markers, ending at side edge. *Continued overleaf*

Shape Shoulder.

S.s. over first 12 (14, 14, 15, 15) sts., work to end and fasten off.

With right side of work facing, miss centre 14 (14, 17, 17, 20) sts., rejoin yarn and pattern to end. Work to match first side, reversing all shaping.

Sleeves (Both Alike).

With 3.50 mm crochet hook, make 31 (31, 33, 33, 36) ch. Work in d.c. as for Back for 7 cm, 2¾ inches. [30 (30, 32, 32, 35) d.c.]

Increase row. — 1 ch., 1 d.c. in same place as ch., 2 d.c. in each of next 9 (7, 7, 6, 7) d.c., 3 d.c. in each of next 11 (14, 16, 19, 19) d.c., 2 d.c. in each of last 9 (8, 8, 6, 8) d.c. [71, (74, 80, 83, 89) d.c.]

Next row. — 1 ch., 1 d.c. in each d.c. to end.

Work in V tr. pattern (see abbreviations) throughout until sleeve measures 43 cm, 17 inches, from beginning. Lengthen or shorten here if required.

Fasten off.

The Neckband.

Join shoulder seams.

With right side of work facing, starting at right back edge, work 30 (32, 32, 34, 34) d.c. across back neck and 56 (56, 60, 60, 64) d.c. evenly round front neck, s.s. to first d.c. to join, turn. [86 (88, 92, 94, 98) d.c.]

1st row. — 1 ch., 1 d.c. in each d.c. to end, s.s. into first ch., turn.

2nd row. — 1 ch., work in d.c. throughout, decrease 3 sts. evenly across back neck and 6 sts. evenly across front neck, s.s. to first ch., turn.

3rd row. — As 2nd row, decreasing 2 sts. evenly across back neck and 6 sts. evenly across front neck.

4th row. — As 2nd row, decreasing 4 sts. evenly across front neck, s.s. to first ch. and fasten off.

To Make Up.

Matching centre of sleeves to shoulder seams and sleeve edges to marked edges of body, sew in sleeves. Join sleeve and side seams.

Lightly press neckband only, do not press remainder. ■

Continued from page 171

Fergus shot her a triumphant look. He was jubilant — she'd used his name at last!

"I'm perfectly possible," he told her. Much more possible, he added to himself, than that wretched Reilly fellow who'd run off to a better job. Thank goodness *he* was out of the way.

Someone else was pushing past them to the sink. He followed Sally back to her easel, and waited while she collected her painting gear.

"What about our portraits?" said Sally.

"Leave them where they are," Fergus told her. "Who wants portraits when they've got the real thing?

"Look, it's only nine o'clock and there's a coffee bar round the corner that stays open till ten. Would you — er —?"

He stopped and waited.

"It's still raining," faltered Sally. "And I haven't an umbrella. I really think I'd better . . ."

Fergus stopped her excuses. "I've got an umbrella. An outsize one. Big enough for two."

And I hope it keeps on raining till after ten, he thought joyfully. Especially when I've got an umbrella big enough for two.

——————— * **THE END** * ———————